DIARIES OF A DEPRESSED TEENAGER

DIARIES OF A DEPRESSED TEENAGER

MIA RAYNA

DIARIES OF A DEPRESSED TEENAGER

iUniverse books may be ordered through booksellers or by contacting:

iUniverse
1663 Liberty Drive
Bloomington, IN 47403
www.iuniverse.com
1-800-Authors (1-800-288-4677)

ISBN: 978-1-5320-0575-6 (sc)
ISBN: 978-1-5320-0576-3 (e)

Library of Congress Control Number: 2016914130

Print information available on the last page.

iUniverse rev. date: 02/23/2017

DEDICATION

I'd like to dedicate this book to my family. Not just because I used them so freely in my writing, but because I truly don't know where I'd be without them.

LET'S START WITH WHY?

It was sometime in the eighth grade that I saw my very first therapist and even though that was our first and last appointment together, she gave me "homework" that turned into an outlet I carried throughout my young life. She told me I should start writing down everything I was feeling or thinking on a daily basis, in a journal where I could be 100% honest and be able to reflect of some things I may not have even known about myself.

Daily was a stretch, but in time I did start writing somewhat regularly in my free time.

Maybe this goes without saying, but I've learned *a lot*. What I didn't expect is that it wasn't all about myself.

See the thing I learned about myself was that I undoubtedly have depression and anxiety. I also learned I undoubtedly have attention deficient disorder and obsessive-compulsive disorder, but those are separate issues.

What I learned about my depression was that it all seemed very internal, even when it wasn't. I had gotten too comfortable in my own head and it made it more and more difficult for me to get out, especially when I really needed to. Everything I dealt with seemed like it was all coming from me, directed at me, and never going to leave me. It was like how a shy person reacts around new people. The more people there are, the quieter they get. The more I needed to be free of myself, the more lost I would get. I never felt more isolated than when I was in my darkest places. Those were the times I was the most lost and something kept holding me back, like the little girl from *Insidious* in that weird black hole thing. What I'm saying is: writing everything down made me realize that some of my problems had a lot to do with how I interacted with the entire rest of the world and vise versa and that was a discovery that changed a lot for me.

I learned that I couldn't change every last thing about myself and even though it drove me crazy, that was okay because at the very least I could change how it affected me and in turn, how I could choose to use it. I learned to get out of myself more often in situations I otherwise would've never enjoyed and when they didn't I learned to utilize *that* time as the time to be internal. In these times, I would write.

So for the next five years, I wrote. I wrote at all hours of the day and night, to all different types of music from Carrie Underwood to Drake, I wrote while I traveled and while I cried, in all different places like my room or Time Square, I wrote until I literally couldn't anymore because of how numb my hand was. I would write everything, no matter how stupid or insignificant it seemed at the time because after a while, I realized nothing that randomly popped into my head was insignificant. I would write for myself, for my school assignments and sometimes what I wrote for myself would later become my assignments. I wrote like my life depended on it because at some points I know it did.

With that, five years later I wrote until I had a crazy idea. An idea to take every last thing I'd written down all these years and use it for something I knew I could. I knew that if I did absolutely nothing else of importance in my life, I would send a message to every last person in the world who felt ever felt like me, even for a second and if I could, I would save lives.

I know that may sound dramatic, but it was really all I thought of every time I tried to talk myself out of it, which I did *a lot*. It was an idea I threw around in my head for awhile before I finally decided to act on it and after that, there was just no turning back. I had set my mind on something and I was doing it for reasons I was very clear on.

I know I'm not perfect. To this day, I carry my demons and I don't have all the answers, but sometimes I found comfort in people who could listen and really understand what I was saying and feeling. That's what I thought of every time I felt like quitting.

So why did I decide to write an entire book of the most depressing things a person can possible think of? I could come up with a million beautifully fluffy reasons about why I started writing this that would sound much better than the actual truth, but I'm a hopelessly honest person so the honest answer is, I didn't. The truth is this literally started as a diary and nothing more.

The deed was pretty much done, but I still had to double and triple check on a pretty much regular basis that this decision was absolutely what I wanted and not something I would live to regret.

The answer was never the same. Sometimes I was sure beyond any doubt that this was the right decision and other times I wondered if what I'd started should stay as it started: personal. I also wondered if maybe I was being too honest at times and if that would later come back to bite me in the ass. I frequently had to reread entries and decide if it was better to omit them or edit them to sound less harsh or brutal. In the early stages *a lot* was omitted and *a lot* was altered. Later on, I decided to include everything exactly as it was and I mean everything. By the end, nothing was left untold or ignored and absolutely nothing was filtered. If I was going to share something I was going to share it exactly how I thought it, without any restrictions.

That's ultimately how I came to the decision to publish my diary anonymously. I had to be at least somewhat conscious of other people's feelings and privacy. I found it gave me so much more freedom in my decision-making when I didn't have to worry about who I mentioned or possibly offended. I could literally say anything, which is usually what I'd do in my day-to-day life anyway. Everything became more authentic and personal to me and I imagined it would do the same for whoever would read these thoughts and not have me to interpret them (which could sometimes be necessary.)

As hard as it may be to believe, never in all the time I spent slaving away over pieces of paper writing my deepest, craziest thoughts did I ever think anyone but me would ever see this stuff. As a matter of fact, for a while the idea of anyone else reading any of it literally petrified me. Every thing you read in this book is something I wrote at any random moment in my life that I had something to get off my chest. It's all my truest, deepest, 100% authentic thoughts. *This is my diary* and only now did it also become yours.

TIME

3/21/12

Time is something I, like most people, complain to never have and yet when we find ourselves with nothing to do, do nothing with it.

Here I find myself looking out into space wondering what to do with the next two hours of my Friday detention. Then that thought pulls me to think of all the things I always say I would do more if I had the time.

Workout? Not here.

Learn a new skill? Probably against the rules.

Develop a clear thoroughly thought out plan for my future? Who am I kidding?

Of all my limited options and resources, writing seemed the most realistic.

When this detention started at exactly 3:01pm, our teacher handed out a blank piece of paper along with another paper that had a picture of a lion on it. I'm no genius, but I'm pretty sure the expectation was for us to draw/trace the lion onto the blank paper which is pretty much what most of the other kids in the detention chose to do as entertainment.

That was the only thing that separated me from any of the other kids in this class that had broken a rule. When the class had started I had asked for lined paper, just so I could write.

Write what? No clue.

See I'm plagued with the same disease you may be familiar with.

Procrastination.

I constantly tell myself that I'll write something incredible later.

When? When I have the time.

I guess it's good news then that I now have two hours to write about all those things I've already forgotten about. Ouch.

So here we are.

I've written so much already that my hand is already starting to feel the pain of my young carpel tunnel. It must be some kind of ironic that someone who loves to write suffers from a condition that causes pain when writing. I also have ADD, which is why I'm naming diseases I have, but that have nothing to do with whatever it is I'm talking about. What was I talking about?

It's already 4:00pm. Time is moving faster than my hand is.

That's a good topic. Moving on. Something I don't know how to do.

I'm sorry; I realize I'm rambling. I really wish I could tell you that during this detention I discovered some grand universal truth about life, but unfortunately, I haven't. I think my biggest talent is that I can see shit for what it is. Sometimes that allows me to give some really fabulous advice, but that's about it.

Sometimes I think I'm bordering on some really amazing breakthrough and then I remember; I'm just a teenager. Another teenager that suffers from ADD and an overactive imagination.

Right now, I'm imagining what would happen if a plane crashed into this classroom right now and this paper (assuming paper wasn't extremely flammable) was all they found. No name, no date, not even a gender, just the random ramblings of an unknown teenager.

Realistically, I know that would never happen. After the initial explosions, there would be nothing left to show for the pain in my head or my hand. So basically, I'm screwed.

You'd turn on your TV and see a report of the tragedy and a list of all the poor victims names would pass before your eyes and you would never think twice when the screen passed mine. Who am I? To you or to anyone. No one. You could look at it all and think "wow that's sad," if that, and then move on about your day without wasting too much time.

You would never know which of those dead kids were kind, happy, mean, rude, or sad. They would all just be grouped together under one tragedy you're lucky you weren't a part of. You, the viewer, would never know which kid picked lined paper instead of drawing paper to a drawing someone else already drew.

Seriously though, what kind of teacher would promote such little creativity in a bunch of students? "Here, go copy this picture of someone else's work cause you'll never do anything on your own?" Looking around this room, it could definitely true for some people in here, but damn. At least give us the blank paper and let us try to use some imagination. At least pretend your trying to make us more rounded people.

Ouch. There goes the carpel tunnel again.

I'm sitting here thinking at least I'm trying to be creative no matter how much it literally pains me and then I look up to see the kid next to me has completely fallen asleep in the middle of copy-drawing his lion. That's exactly how boring I'd imagined the task would be.

That being said how is anyone suppose to feel hopeful and/or special growing up in a generation like this.

The colder than this room truth about it is, they're not.

Is changing this even possible? I guess I'll never know if I keep finding myself surrounded by a bunch of sleep-drawers, drawing from other people's creativity. Too suppressed to even imagine their own creative potential, forget fulfill it.

I may only be another sickened, saddened teenager, but my brain is still functional and it's plagued with this disease that I call opinion and one separate from all other things that could cloud my vision like it clouds my neighbors vision besides his eyelids. My eyes have also fallen ill because they are tortured with sight that allows for conscious, knowing and willing vision to see what most others ignore.

I've spent my entire life this far seeing, learning, and questioning only to realize, as a teenager no less, that there are no answers.

There are no explanations. There are no legitimate reasons we are all meant to live by the standards that "silence is golden," or that "ignorance is bliss," because that is our truest disease. Ignorance.

We are so afraid of what we don't know that we don't even want to know it.

I'll never understand it and I probably never will. Another question to go unanswered.

People talk so much about how badly they want to see change, but that's all they're willing to do. Talk and watch.

Is it wrong to say that I don't even want to live in a world like this? Would it be wrong to insinuate that maybe all the teenagers that have taken their own lives have done so because their lives were never truly given to them to begin with?

I frequently think about what the world would look like without me and to be honest, it looks the same. I think that's kind of the problem, but it's also one of the top reasons I haven't done it.

Nothing would change.

I would just be another name on a screen representing another victim and I would hate to be remembered as nothing more than that. That's not who I am and I never want anyone to think it is. That's the only thing that scares me more than riding this out. I refuse to let anyone but me decide what I'll be remembered as and I certainly am not allowing "weak" or "victim" to even come into consideration.

I am plagued like any other human being on this earth, but am also victim to several man-made diseases I think we all share.

STRAIGHT FACTS

1. There are 7.3 billion people living on this planet today.
2. America alone makes up 318.86 million of those people.
3. These numbers have and are projected to continue to incline by the billions in the not so distant future.

How could it be then that the total number of youth in America has and is projected to continue to *decline* over the next several years? By youth, I mean that sector of America that still attends schools, gets claimed on tax returns, and often falls under the title of "juvenile."

There's no definitive answer, of course, but as we know well in this country, it's probably most effective to come to a conclusion first and find facts to back up our opinions later.

Let's say I like to work backwards. So here're some more facts.

4. More people of all ages are depressed and suicidal today than ever before in the history of this country.

5. More children at younger ages are displaying symptoms of depression and children who display these symptoms will more than likely carry them into adulthood, more so if overlooked throughout childhood.

6. As the 10th leading cause of death in America, more than 40,000 people commit suicide every year. It is the 2nd leading cause among Americans between the ages of 10-24, making it 1.8x the national average.

This isn't a research paper so don't get scared prematurely. I swear I have a point.

See the fact here is, this isn't about troubled teens and why the world should be completely fixated on them and their "juvenile" problems. Despite what you may think, most of us "juveniles" don't crave that much attention, quite the opposite actually. Most of us usually try to get by under the radar because we're made to believe everything we do is wrong. Maybe that's just me.

Regardless, this isn't about any of that. This is about the cost of those facts. Not just economically – which is an estimated $44 billion in the U.S. each year – but nationally - emotionally.

This is about me because this is also about you. This is about us. The highly dismissed group of "troubled youth" that accounted for 22.9% of American people in

2015. A statistic that would only haunt you like it does me if you knew that this number has gotten lower and lower every year since 1966 and is projected to continue to do so. And even greater than that, the growing number of people in general that deal with what we have.

Why should you care? Mostly because that declining number also represents the equally rapid and certain decline of the future we're suppose to play a pretty big part in.

Unless the plans have changed, one day in said upcoming future, we will make up the other percentage of that same population and traditionally of course, make the same mistakes. But also because somewhere in that statistic is represented someone you know or love. Perhaps someone you never even knew was in need of help because they themselves didn't know.

This would only haunt you if you were as invested in that statistic and those people like I am.

Maybe you forgot, but this is the same group people you did or do belong to at one point, just like your children are and just like their children also will be. So what type of world are you leaving behind for them? What type of world are you living in?

A world of separate groups categorized by numbers and statistics. The number you are known as a social but is anything but or the number in your bank account and where that leaves you in relation to the rest of the world.

We are a number, nothing more than a percentage. We are *that* percentage and we are the future, but we have to be here to build it.

7. Juvenile:

- Of or relating to or characteristics of or appropriate for children or young people.
- Displaying or suggesting a lack of maturity
- Not fully developed

R.I.P MR. WALLACE

11/17/15

"It is not the least bit coincidental that adults who commit suicide with firearms almost always shoot themselves in the head. They shoot the terrible master. And the truth is that most of these suicides are actually dead long before they pull the trigger."

– David Foster Wallace

That was a quote by David Foster Wallace from a famous speech he made back in 2008, the same year my parents got divorced. Weird coincidence I guess, that 8 years later I'd discover all the things he was saying during the time I was thinking it.

I listened to this speech one time by accident and read it repeatedly for about a month, but I read this particular part of it over and over again. The thing that stuck out to me most was his views on thought. Basically that your own thoughts are trying to kill you and they have better chances of succeeding than anything or anyone else on

Gods green earth. He's dead now so I think he was speaking from experience. Not to be morbid, but he'd suffered from depression am anxiety just like me most of his life and inevitably ended up killing himself. Which only makes the whole thing even more interesting to me.

It's actually a really crazy concept when you think about it. How your thoughts can rule you or how your thoughts basically are you.

Everything I am is all just in my own head. My entire personality, everything that makes me, me and everything I know is all just what's in between my ears. It doesn't matter what I look like or really what anyone looks like because in essence we all just look like the same mushy brain and in the end we all just ended up looking like the same skeleton.

I'm don't really think that's the point that Wallace was trying to get across but that's what I took from it. It kind of changed my whole view on a lot of things ... again. It took a lot to get me to care about trivial things before but now I'm confident that it would be next to impossible to make me feel insecure about pretty much anything.

Before you dismiss me, know this is isn't about my personal insecurities, though they are plentiful.

I've gone through a lot of weird phases in my juvenile life. When I was the embodiment of everything you'd expect of a sociopathic delinquent, I would imagine what it would be like to die in different ways. It's not like I planned to test out any of the theories, this was just the point in my life when I realized that no matter what I would have to die one day and figured I should consider which way I'd most prefer.

Anyway, I always used to say that getting shot in the head would probably be the quickest, least painful way to go. Now I wonder if this was all just my little devil speaking to me.

I think that's what this is really all about. The whole fantasy that there's a little angel and a little devil on each of your shoulders thing came right from this idea. The idea that there's something living inside you that both wants to love you and destroy you like a bipolar schizophrenic you can't even run from. That thought is enough to drive someone crazy, but then I guess that would mean it's doing its job.

I think Mr. Wallace and I are spiritually related. He said all this stuff about allowing your thoughts to take over and then he let them do it to him. I do it too so I don't really have a ledge to stand on, but just like him, I know talking about the devil and outing his tactics doesn't take away any of his power. It just subconsciously fuels his existence, like tinker bell.

"They shoot the terrible master. And the truth is that most of these suicides are actually dead long before they pull the trigger." Dead long before they pull the trigger.

HOW I RAISED MYSELF

I was nine years old when I became a parent. When I felt like I was thirty-nine and going through a midlife crisis. Nine years old when I sat across from the man that was supposed to be my parent and had the roles between guardian and child reversed. I was nine years old when my life turned upside down and then went on to spiral out of control right up until now.

I was nine when my father told me he and my mother's relationship was over - or that it had never really begun and though it wasn't breaking news to me that they were unhappy, I can admit that hearing it and watching it actually play out in front of me was an experience that I otherwise wouldn't or couldn't admit changed me.

I was in middle school when they finally made the decision to go their separate ways. They told me they'd only waited that long because they wanted to give me time to get older. I'm 100% sure that only made it worse because I was only old enough to know and understand what was happening, not cope with it.

I still remember the day my dad alone took me out to eat at one of my favorite places in our little town and told me like it was nothing. I cried all over my chicken fingers for the rest of that outing. Our waitress had worked there for years; she's actually a manager there now. Every time I go back I remember the little smile she kept giving me that day since it was pretty obvious I was a little emotional. That isn't one of my favorite places anymore.

Looking back on it now, I always wonder why my mom wasn't there. Their relationship, their divorce, and even their interactions to this day all run by a very divided task concept. You do this and I'll do that. I'd never noticed it before but once I did, I wondered if that was the reason my mom wasn't there that day. You'd think that would be at least one thing they could do together.

Your probably trying to figure out why this matters and so was I, but trust me it does. It was these little things that stuck to me and made me who I am now. Relationships aren't my thing, not that I haven't tried. I just severely dislike the idea of sharing my life when it should only be mine and I alone can guarantee it. I refuse to let anyone have power of how I feel in a day, especially when I barely control that to begin with. I have a love/hate relationship with team work because I expect teamwork to mean actually working together on all fronts and not dividing tasks and being told what yours are.

I'm not saying I'm damaged eternally because my parents couldn't work together because I've long since accepted that fact. I'm saying all those years I wondered about the little abnormalities in my head I never thought or really wanted to look back at where they may have come from, but when I did I found way more plausible answers than I ever had before.

I'd be lying if I said it was easy because it definitely wasn't. There were many nights I tortured myself writing about all the things I could remember from my childhood. I would cry alone for hours, but sometimes it was kind of therapeutic for me. Take that as you wish.

It's obvious that all kids eventually have to face the realities of life, but for most people it's probably not a process that they could recall and explain to someone vividly. The way I had to face my realities didn't allow me that luxury.

I used to say I thought our family was so lucky because nothing bad ever happened to us. I remember saying it to my mom one day when we were walking in New York like it just happened. I remember her never agreeing or disagreeing with me. Sometimes she'd laugh but that was pretty much it. I was ignorant then, that's probably why she never acknowledged me when I said it. She knew better than I did at the time. I was so sheltered and I was the only one who didn't know it so when things weren't so blissfully perfect, I thought I jinxed the shit out of us. Now I know better too.

So I'll admit I have always been a shameless daddy's girl. Everyone that knows us knows that I am my father's clone and for that we grew an inseparable closeness that swayed both ways on the lines between parent and friend.

The problem was that most often he was more a friend than a father, especially post divorce. My father quite frankly fell apart after his and my mother's relationship did. I saw something in him visibly change and for me that was one of the scariest, most humbling things I've ever had to see. The man I idolized, falling apart.

As a father, he was everything you would imagine and more. He held me when I cried, gave me everything I wanted and stood in my room when I was scared at night. Still as spoiled as I may sound, it felt like I lost everything when I lost this. Suddenly, I was the one who had to hold him when he cried, and be brave in the dark. I had lost my rock and my idol and for a while it made me lose myself.

I know how this sounds, but to be honest I don't think there is a better way to explain why things that other people can put out of their minds cut me so deeply. Disappointment wasn't just an emotion for me; it was a weapon for my own and only destruction, like rat poison. I consciously set my expectations low so I could never experience it or at least minimize our encounters because this one emotion crushed me. The problem is disappointment comes in all forms and some just aren't escapable. I grew up watching the society that raised me screw over almost everyone I know and loved. This society ruined my family and that is no exaggeration.

Financial stability is the #1 reason most people get married and it's also the #1 reason most people get divorced (aside from avoidable things like infidelity.) It's the #1 thing most people strive for in life and it's the only thing that could destroy them if they don't.

This was a fact that played out in my home, but I also watched it happen to so many homes I'd encountered.

Two of my middle school friends parents got divorced, and two of my cousins parents have remained in unhappy marriages just for the financially stability. A friend I have right now, spends most of her free time in the local precinct with her mom and her boyfriend, but she'd never leave him for fear of losing, you guessed it, financial stability.

The system we have allowed ourselves to live by is what ruined my perception of family, of love, and unity. It took me about 10 years to figure those things out again, and I'm not even sure I have.

★   ★   ★   ★   ★

I read an article once that spoke on human ego. It said in a nutshell that most people view themselves as being different or more special than everyone else. Though I'm sure this is absolutely true, I believe that some people actually are. Not always the people who claim to be for whatever superficial reason, but I do think that certain people really are different, mentally. I believe that some people think differently and that enables them to experience life differently and feel things differently.

Despite all of my father's heartaches: his divorce, losing his job and his house he has never lost his sense of humor. He has never failed to be the same person that made me laugh at nine years old or at seventeen. He taught me how to see the good things in life through the bad, the importance of family and its support. He gave equal importance to setting big goals and surpassing them despite obstacles.

Simply by being himself, he taught me how to think individually and to voice those thoughts even when people or he himself disagreed. For this I know he is one of those special people and he's allowed me to think like one too.

I was given a rare blessing in being able to call a person like this my parent and to even begin to see life through his eyes. Don't get me wrong there were many times he was the farthest thing wrong optimistic but then I'm glad it forced me to be for him.

Though I may not be the same person I was seven years ago, I also know that I'm not even the same person I was last year and I definitely won't be the same person I am now even in another seven years, but that is all I hope for.

4/13/14

I've always found something incredibly fascinating about innocence. Something poetic in an ignorant mind like the incentive of tears before we are taught to control them and how universal they can be.

Kids embody everything that is innocence, but our minds, the way we've been taught to use them, can't help but imagine when that innocence will end and what will be the cause.

Through everything I have experienced in my short life, my most prominent thought is how thankful I am for the mind I've developed. I am thankful because while most kids were learning the basics of things they'll never use, I received an entire curriculum of far more useful lessons. I learned lessons that altered me at key points in my development and I genuinely don't think I'd be the same person if I hadn't. I wish everyone could have that. I don't mean I hope everyone's parents get divorced or they experience a lot of bad shit. I mean I wish everyone had someone who could mold their lows into something they could use in their highs, or their other lows.

I have always valued school as a place to better yourself, but I have also never imagined one single building to be a place for education. I am fascinated by what people are capable of and that we are the only species capable of it. The power of the five senses or the human brain even if only 10 percent of it. I have an endless list of questions and curiosities to last lifetimes and I know it all came from the way I grew up.

I grew to know nothing is finite, easily explained, or guaranteed. Things change as do people and we have to learn to adjust to those changes. You could do everything right and have everything go wrong. I think I chose to be a psychology major because of all of it. I couldn't imagine anything else to be the reason. I hope to graduate with more than a diploma because I want to be remembered for more than the name on it.

WHAT A PITY

I could spend hours wallowing in my own self-pity. It became a true talent of mine.

I was remarkably good at sitting alone in dark rooms for hours and listing to no end all the things I hated about myself, about my life, about the world. The list was usually made up of really stupid stuff because the truth is I didn't have much to be upset about I just always was.

Still, I could sit for hours and hate everything because once I had made the decision to be hateful, there was no going back. I had so much anger and hate built up inside me that allowing any of it out was like opening up the flood gates for the epitome of crazy which is why most of the time I chose not to let any of it out at all.

Sometimes it felt like if I did I could think or do crazy things I'd otherwise never do because they lacked my built in ability to overly reason and rationalize.

But this wasn't me and I was genuinely afraid of this person I could become. I was afraid that she had come to existence at all and that the only thing I really knew about her was how angry, sad, and hateful she could be.

Even still I pitied her. I felt so bad for the girl that was literally drowning in herself and how I allowed her to teach me that there was no one around who even remotely cared to save her.

I pitied the girl who felt like she couldn't cry freely and bottled every emotion God gave her like it was a sin to release it or to scream for help when she truly needed it. I pitied the girl who was stuck in quick sand she couldn't get out of and I pitied the girl who sat alone in dark rooms and cried until she couldn't any more as she watched the world speed around her idle body.

I pitied that girl because I knew in the world we lived in, she wouldn't last very long because I knew the world we lived in was built to make sure people like her didn't.

I tried to imagine what a future for me would like it, but nothing ever really appeared. The future was none existent to me. Not because I didn't want one, but because *I really couldn't see on.*

It hurts my heart that we are born with nothing but blank space and infinite possibilities but are doomed from the moment we breathe *this* air. It hurts me so much that people are meant to be incredible creatures, yet usually fall victim to a fucked up mentality that infests our minds like a parasite. It made me so angry that the need to survive always seems to outweigh the importance of living. That learning to speak and understand words is the first chip at our divine destiny because it enables us to be close minded or worse to be able to listen and understand all the negative shit that's surrounding us.

I could spend hours wallowing at a number of things, and I did. And in no time I would find myself wondering whom it was I even pitied anymore because they all looked the same.

1/20/14

Sometimes I forget that my dad moved back in with us after my parents divorced.

You know that thing you hear about people actually deleting memories from their head that they don't want to remember. I think I did that.

My dad moved into a house in the same town as us because he wanted us to be close and spend time with him. He spent thousands of dollars and weeks making this house into a home me and my sister would love just as much as our first one. Not en a few years later, he lost it.

His brother died and it led to him losing his job, not long after, he was back home, but he and my mom were still very divorced. Now this house didn't feel like a home to me either.

I remember him being there during Obamas first election. We all watched history play out of our TV and my sister screamed about all dramatic as she usually does and for a moment in my history, I realized that this would never be real. Our family was no longer a family and therefore, I could no longer pretend it was.

When my mom asked me if I wanted him to stay, I was the one who said I wanted him to leave. Shortly after, she asked him to leave. To this day it hurts me. I love my dad and I never wanted to hurt him, but having him there became too unbearable to me. It felt like something it wasn't and I knew he felt the same way.

The day he confronted me about it I literally wanted to die. He was so hurt the look on his face and the sound in his voice will forever be burned my memory.

My mom's mom was the one that told him. The divorce caused this weird rivalry that was basically that whole side of my family against him. They were the only family he'd had and just like they all turned on him. That's why I've always been aggressively defensive of him. If I didn't, no one else would be. I knew he was far from perfect, but none of that was a fair reason for him to be so isolated that way after everything he'd done for them.

He was alone and for that I would fight with my blood till the day I died for him because he would've done it for me.

My own grandmother had thrown me under the bus just to win a battle and in that moment, no one cared how I would feel. I felt like I'd never make up to him how I'd made him feel when he heard her shove that in his face. She doesn't know it but I still resent her for it sometimes.

This man raised me, confided in me as I'd done with him. When I felt like no one else cared I knew he did and I'd broken him. To this day I feel like I owe him my life for it. Just writing about it makes me cry.

It got to a point that even my sister hated how much I defended him and it had nothing to do with loving him more than my mother because had the roles been reversed I would've done the exact same thing. The fact is she had many allies where he had none, except for me. I knew she would always have someone to love and support her and I would too, but my father didn't. I knew what it felt like to be isolated and I wouldn't wish it on anyone, much less my parent.

FIRST RANT OF THE DAY

3/8/13

I've been going to a therapist as long as I could remember. Every time I expressed my feelings to someone I trusted, I was redirected to a stranger who I was expected to open up to. I was basically being told "do and say what you just did, but say it to this person who I'm paying to listen."

It took me far too long after putting aside far too much pride to tell people I thought I could trust that I was going through ... something, only for them to send me to strangers.

To tell them that I was struggling, that I always had been and that I didn't see it changing anytime soon took everything in me. Not really losing it after, took even more.

I could never look at someone I love, cry the way I did to people this past weekend, and tell them " I think you should talk to someone," especially since I thought that's what I was doing. This was the first time I decided that I really couldn't take it anymore and that isolation wasn't helping.

This was the time I realized that these people, who I considered my last resort, wouldn't be able to help me either.

In one weekend they'd made everything seem impossibly worse. Now, I not only had the same problems I started with, but I now knew the only help that I would get was from a stranger who is essentially getting paid to hear me bitch so no one else would have to.

Refusal of this "help" wasn't even an option because then I would also be accused of not trying to help myself.

So I sat there and told this lady with this consistently blank look on her face my problems. She gave me "homework" I'm not going to do because looking at a half cup of water wasn't what I'd call a resolution. Neither was pill popping, at least not for me. I'd found better "coping" tools on Wikipedia and if I wanted to take pills I could've got them from the sketchy kids at my school.

It seems that what this blank face lady fails to understand is I don't want to cope. I want to be happy and I don't think that's a large request.

I've spent my whole life trying to help myself so no one else would have to and this weekend I found out this is how I would continue to spend the rest of my life, assuming I could of course.

Everyday just got more and more difficult and I don't think it all really had to do with chemicals in my head being imbalanced, though I know it played a huge role. It was knowing everyday that it wasn't getting better that made *it all worse. I had exhausted all my resources, I was now seeing my second or third therapist and after years of just talking all she had left to say to me was "I think you should talk to a psychiatrist."*

BLOOD OR WATER

7/28/13

Maybe I'm making excuses for my own bad habits like they say. They would know better wouldn't they? It makes perfect sense that an older wiser mind could tell me more about how my mind works than I ever could.

Honestly, all I've ever really wanted were answers and ideally real solutions, but mostly answers. Answers to everything I'd felt my entire life because I knew for a fact it wasn't "normal."

See, the people around me particularly, resulted to focusing on all my "bad habits" and picking at those instead. For that, I am given countless answers I didn't ask for.

So what would you make of a drowning sadness that expresses itself in anger? Grades declining just as quickly as my moods? A lack of desire to do pretty much anything including holding basic conversations?

Nothing. Nothing they knew could give me answers to those questions, but naturally they formed their own answers for discussion among themselves.

I used to hate these people, but with time, I understood that the only thing a person who has no idea how to live in your shoes can do, is mock them.

Some of these people I've been around my whole life, others don't know me through a hole in the wall. I don't think I am able or allowed to hate them, despite the fact that hate has become the emotion I'm most comfortable with. I couldn't be mad at people who couldn't answer questions I didn't even have the answers to.

For that, I even hated myself sometimes. Sometimes for no reason at all, but most of the time I'd find one.

I know now, most of the hate came from the sadness. I was angry with anyone who couldn't help me, even when that person was me. How could I put that on anyone? I wanted answers from people that I couldn't even provide for myself. I had to keep reminding myself of that or I would've pushed away everyone I knew. I couldn't always, and I lost more people than I could count because of it, but I still wouldn't consider them all "losses." I'm not difficult to get along with I just expect people to act to certain way that they should want anyway. I know no ones perfect, even I faltered, but I always recognized my mistakes at least so why was something even like that so difficult for some people?

Regardless, arguing and overall problem solving became pointless to me at some point in high school. I didn't have the time or energy to put into stupid shit so if it wasn't making me better, I wasn't involved.

That being said I would've cut myself off at certain points if I could. I would beg myself for help, for answers, so that I could at least help myself.

At this point, I'd allowed everyone to make me believe that if I could reason with myself, I could begin to find my own salvation, I couldn't. All around the board.

I would've saved myself if no one else could, but I couldn't and it made me feel a claustrophobia like no other. I was so trapped within myself. My biggest feuds and arguments were with myself. That the sole reason I never have time for anyone else's problems with me.

I've never felt so hopeless and broken and these feelings were exactly what pushed me further and further into myself.

Everyone else seems so "normal" and all those normal people can't even see how abnormal I am or they didn't care. That also added to my isolation.

Physically I guess I look and act the same, so I cant really blame anyone but myself. Outwardly, I portrayed my father's sense of humor and my mother's thick skin, but inside? I am completely unrecognizable to myself. I don't actually know who I am and at this point in the game I know I should.

So what do I really want from all these people I'm so mad at? Do I want them to stop their worlds so they can suffer in mine? No, but what I do know is I envy their happiness, regularly. It's horrible to admit but I know I do.

How is it fair for all of them to live seemingly perfect, happy lives and I had to live so unexplainably, emotionally deficient. I unjustly compared it to people living in poverty while other people had more money than they knew what to do with. I know there's no comparison because I'm not living in poverty, but do you at least see common denominator here?

Truth be told, a horrible side of me secretly wanted everyone to feel like me, though I'd never act on it, so I could feel normal or at least not alone. The other side of me stared at their happiness and begged them to pull me up with them. Neither was a realistic or healthy way of thinking.

Everything just seems so difficult and confusing that I can't even determine what it is exactly I want even for myself right now.

I want people to care enough to help me, but I work so hard to hide my feelings. How could I expect relief to come when I myself didn't know who or what I wanted it from?

It's just amazing to me that anyone could think that I would want to live like this. Like I genuinely enjoy it. I don't know what twisted world you live in - wait yes I do - but I would do anything to just as simply as you make it seem, save myself. At some points I would've died for it.

SEPTEMBER ELEVENTH

9/11/13

Today was exactly what I expected it to be. Class after class of learning about the history of this day over and over.

I know I probably sound like a morbid bitch right now, but you would too if you had to spend a whole day watching documentaries about people dying or other people talking about those people dying.

I have all the sympathy and compassion in the world for the people who suffered and still suffer from the events of that day.

Truth be told, I didn't personally lose anyone close to me, but in the moment I knew both my parents worked in New York and I was a middle school student there. I knew exactly what fear and chaos it caused, and I was terrified. My family lived all over the city and even at my young age I knew I should be. My uncle picked me up from school and I went to my cousin's house to watch my city fall apart on NY1.

My point being: I don't really have a place to say I was bored listening to them talk about it all day. The only thing I'd truly lost was a childhood fantasy of New York being the most untouchable city in the world.

Even if I had lost someone close, I can't honestly say I would've been anymore excited to hear about it at this point.

People are dealing with just as much devastation everyday all over the world but no one hear seems to stop and acknowledge their pain. Not while it's happening and definitely not on that day every year basically forever.

So why should a school completely stop teaching to "educate" students on the same things we already know about?

It was a morbid topic and I was morbid enough on my own.

In addition, most of what I learned was about the facts and the statistics. They would tell you all about how many minutes it took each tower to fall and how many people died but not who those people were. I saw countless politicians talk about what happened even though they weren't even there, but I never really saw the face or heard the story of the people that were.

So although my first class I was wholly interested, it didn't last long. I wanted to see the rawest footage of what really happened to the city that bore me. If you haven't noticed, civic involvement is kind of my thing. That I did see, for an entire day.

By the second class, I was far less interested. I had to sit through another 45 minutes of the exact same videos that were already burned into my brain. At this point, I'd resorted to people watching.

I watched all the other kids in my class watch the videos. Unsurprisingly, most of them weren't. I figured it was probably not the same experience for them. They didn't understand how much New York meant to this country and therefore what exactly this event meant to it as well. They weren't born and raised there so to them it was just another tragedy and not even a big enough one to make them look up from the screens of their phones.

By my last class I'd moved on to a whole new method of interpretation entirely.

I've watched the actual footage from this day so many times it's ridiculous. The thing I always remembered most was watching the people jump from the windows to escape the flames. It was the hardest part to forget because it was the hardest part to watch.

At this point I was watching it totally differently. I watched the people jump again like it was the first time I'd ever really seen it.

These people jumped from all the way up there, knowing they're chances of survival were no better, if not worse, than if they stayed in the burning buildings. So why then did they choose to do it?

I suppose for them it wasn't an action of survival but one of self granted mercy. Jump and decide your own fate that you hope to be less painful or ... stay and burn. I guess there was a small amount of hope that they could be rescued but realistically it was clear those chances were small.

Given the circumstances, I guess the choice would be easy.

If someone was in a bad enough situation and it seemed as though the possibility of being rescued was unfavorable small, I would think that person, no matter who they were, how strong minded or willed, would decide to put themselves out of their misery rather than stay on false hope and be burned alive. Stay and burn or jump?

I left school feeling more miserable then when I got there.

I THINK THIS IS LOVE

This is going to sound like a stupid joke, but there was an actual point in my life when I thought I'd forgot how to feel feelings. Let me break that down: I believed that I had trained myself to control my feelings. I would actually make conscious decisions to not let things spark any emotional reaction in me and in most situations I really could. Seriously.

It had gotten to a point that my best friend actually told me she thought I had a disease called alexithymia and that I was infecting her.

Alexithymia is literally defined as a dysfunction in emotional awareness, social attachment, and interpersonal relating.

For dummies: I was a cold-hearted bitch.

I have to laugh at myself cause I swear I'm not an actual psychopath even though that's exactly what I sound like.

If I'm being honest, I don't think I would survive well in this world without this. I didn't handle emotions well. Not my own and definitely not anyone else's. I crumbled under my own pressure and if I worried about anyone else, I crumbled under that too, till I couldn't breath. So I literally *had* to learn to care and show less.

My thoughts are stronger than my entire being. They control me more than I could ever hope of controlling them and that's how it works for everyone. You just are what you think. You see something and you think up a response and that's just how you feel and you don't even really know why. It's just something in your head that sees, and tells you how you feel about it.

My thoughts were my enabler. They allowed me, if not encouraged me, to think about myself all the time. The told me to pity myself, and worry about myself and unless I counter acted those thoughts I would naturally always choose myself over everything else.

My fight vs. flight reaction was pretty much always set to fly and with haste. I had to decide to choose fight and that wasn't something that came easy to me at first.

It was like being in a relationship you know isn't healthy, but can never get out of. I had developed an unhealthy relationship with myself.

It was like I wanted out, but at the same time I felt like there was something that could be saved or that things would change for the better so I would always stay. I would complain and complain, mostly to myself, about how stupid and pathetic I was being, but I would never separate us.

At some point, the relationship became a crutch. In some ways it protected me from the dangers of what was outside my unhappy home, just not from the ones inside. So it brought me to this point, I don't know when this point came, but it was a point that I didn't even want to leave anymore. I would just say I did to make myself feel better.

I had accidently gotten into an abusive relationship but I had knowingly made the choice to marry my abuser.

By "it" I mean my sadness. I had bonded us in such a way that our vows were written in blood and they really meant till death do us part.

AMERICAN PRIDE

My sophomore year of high school, my history teacher asked my class to write an essay about how we show our American pride. I quite nearly flew out of seat right through the roof and not cause I was filled with uncontrollable excitement. Who was this man to tell me I *had* to be prideful of anything. I hated this country. I had no American pride and therefore didn't feel a need to show any pride forward it whatsoever.

After I finished exercising my freedom of speech, I realized I probably overreacted a little. So I decided I would happily do his assignment.

My own way. As always.

This is what I wrote:

What is American pride and how are you supposed to show it? Can you see it just on a person you cross paths with? Is it boastful or humble? If the question is how do you show your American pride, how do you answer? Is that even a question that can be easily answered? No, I don't think it is, at least not for me. America is a country that was built on the promise of freedoms and bravery and yet it has become almost professional in its attempts to cover up the lack of such things. America is a country that resembles a child with so much potential but gives in to the pressures surrounding it.

As a nation, we have set the standards for individual freedoms and overall in our quest to make other countries see the world through what we believe are our own clear eyes. As unfortunate as it seems, what was once a clear picture of an ideal world has now become clouded even to us. Which leaves the question, how can the country that's supposed to set the example for everyone else, remember to always uphold its original promises? Who shows us when we are doing things wrong or when we've begun to sway the wrong way?

We do, the people of America. We were given the right in our original amendments to express our opinions in order to maintain a fair and just society, yet so many of us choose not to. We have relied so heavily on the opinion of others that we ourselves have withheld our own opinions. We each have our own vision usually accompanied by complaints about the way things should be done, but hardly any of us do anything to make those changes.

The beauty of America is that is it the home of American legends that have cared so deeply for the people living here that they have inspired mass change, not only for their self, but for huge groups of people. Incredible leaders like Martin Luther King, Rosa Parks, and Abraham Lincoln have each spearheaded their own revolutions on a small or grand scale even at the risk of their own life, but nonetheless for something they believed in. The problem with America today *is* pride and the problem with American pride is that there is none. Americans have lost their passion and drive to better our country and therefore have ceased to have any pride at all. We have taken our freedoms for granted and therefore have viewed our country as nothing more than the place we live. *We* are the problem. We each seek change that none of us care to invoke. We crave to be heard in a country that has maintained its promise of freedom in exchange for silence. How do Americans show their pride as a posed to how they should? We complain, we get angry and frustrated, and we do nothing.

Americans have become too comfortable in their silence. They have decided that the comfort of oblivion is safer and easier than the cost of pushing change that is necessary. America is beautiful because it is built on and continues to have raw potential that has hardly been explored. I believe in the potential of this country because I believe in the potential of its people even if no one else does.

How do I show American pride? By Acknowledging and accepting its flaws. By recognizing where this country has been, but also envisioning where it could go but most importantly by wanting to be a part in building that future. By being passionate enough to make this country a better home not only for myself but also for every generation that follows me. American pride is more than just a feeling, it is an action and it is us. We each are a symbol of American pride just by being a part of it. The very fact that we call this country our home and call ourselves Americans is because we believe in what it stands for. Although we may not agree with everything, the beauty of America is that we don't have to. We only have to care enough to state our opinion and take action if we want change badly enough.

"I'VE BELIEVED AS MANY AS SIX IMPOSSIBLE THINGS BEFORE BREAKFAST"

4/28/14

We pass hundreds of thousands of people everyday. I think subconsciously, we naturally make our own judgments and forget about it later and it all happens so fast so we don't even really have time to think about it.

When I look at people I most often wonder what they're thinking while I'm thinking what I'm thinking. I'm usually thinking something completely out of this world when someone looks at me even though all they see is resenting bitch face. So what do they automatically think when they see my face? What do they think about in general? How do they view things their world because in their mind the world could be a completely different place.

I know exactly what it looks like to me. I can't go a full minute without thinking or hearing something about my world that genuinely scares me. Today, it was that Obama's Paycheck Fairness Act had been denied. Again. I can't honestly say I'm surprised, but as always, I'm disappointed. I realize it wasn't a world-changing proposition, but that's what scares me more than anything. Something as simple as allowing workers to freely discuss wages and employers to submit more information on their workers wasn't allowed to pass. These small problem solutions that we overlook is where we need to start in order to fix the larger ones so just briefly imagine what something like this means for those larger issues.

I've always been a crazy over thinker. I honestly think its what I do best. I look into things so deeply sometimes it drives me actually crazy and sometimes I swear I've broken some incredible ground on some never before thought of idea.

The world we live in is an idea I think about incessantly. I see normal kids my age all doing exactly what's expected of them: being innocently happy, or typically careless. I wonder how they could be so careless or so happy knowing what's in store for them – for us. How could I hear these things and feel like everyone should be as panicked as I am and look around to find that no one is ... besides me.

We spend "the best years of our lives" in school just so we can end up with a degree that will not only put you in thousands of dollars in depth, but that won't even be able to get a job with, so we may be allowed to spend the rest of lives, hating the previously mentioned non-existent jobs.

Suppose you do get a job and suppose it's a good one. Great? No, not great. Because now you get to spend the rest of your life working to boost an economy for a country that has guaranteed you no retirement money, ensuring that you will work till you die or die from no work. If that takes too long than they will swiftly find another creative way to get rid of you.

What did you expect? The money is gone, but the people keep coming. The debt is piling, but the money keeps being spent. Where exactly do you expect to see the light at the end of the tunnel?

I guess you could always resort to drug dealing. Live in poor city, under inhumane and unsafe circumstances, in fear of the other people who would do just as much to survive as you would, or the same authority to come back and take even more from you than they have because, lets face it, at this point people are fighting to be able to live in those poor cities.

Which all brings me back to my original point. Why are these people so happy? Are they seeing something I'm not? Do they know something I don't? I really doubt it.

Just like the kids they tell us not to act like, they're just playing pretend. Every single person I see is hiding behind their ignorance to protect themselves from really seeing the truth of what's happening. The world is a horrible place and ignoring it isn't making it any better. I can't be happy simply because I live here.

Granted, I know this country's far better off than others, but we're not to far from being just the same and in many ways we already are. How can anyone be so blind or care so little? It's astonishing to me how severely human priority has shifted to *things that couldn't be any less important. Not a single thing will matter if you're living in hell.*

Besides, the obvious fact that humans are ruining our planet I also and mostly mean that humans are ruining humans. Their happiness, their quality of life, their chances.

I think that's a much scarier thought. Global warming and disease will be the least of our worries when you are no longer on the same side of the very species you belong to.

I guess in some weird way I can understand why people have learned to be so carless toward luxuries they abuse on a regular basis. Humans have been breed to believe that they are more important than all things, apparently even more than each other.

Selfishness is a real human disease that is spreading so quickly it's might as well be considered a plague. At times, it even tempted me to be more self-absorbed. If everyone was going to care only for himself or herself than why should I care about anyone else? I can only describe this thought as trying to cure a disease by infecting myself.

From this I dawned on me that if I wanted more people to see things the way I do, I had to think like me, not like other people.

PRESSURE

6/20/14

I want to talk about niches. We're all meant to find ours and attach to it like everyone seems to do, but the idea of it actually gives me really bad anxiety.

Nothing discouraged me more than the pressures of having to conform to the systems set by someone else, specifically society. Nothing seemed more frightening to me than the idea that I was considered to belong to one specific type of people and my job in life was to find it and become a part of it.

There are so many different parts of me that, I suppose, can be categorized in to so many factions that I could never be like just one or even a few ... how could anyone?

Maybe it was just me, but it seemed impossible to do something so blatantly degrading like to say you're no more or no different than a title or a group.

Making friends as a freshman in high school seemed like a scary task enough and I barely succeeded at that and yet here I was about to be a senior, only to find out that I would need to do the same thing all over again, on an even larger scale.

My whole thing here is, despite what anyone may tell you, you'll never really get out of high school. You may not have to go to algebra again but you will forever be stuck in high school in some form. In fact, you're in high school most, if not all of your life, from start to finish. For the entirety of your days you will be asked life altering questions at the most in-opportune times of your life that you alone must decide the answers to. You will always be surrounded by teacher's -good and bad- and you will be forced to learn from them everyday even by accident, even in the smallest ways. You will always need to find your place and know it and even still you will always be tempted to do something you never thought you'd do. Everyday for the rest of your life is a high school experience, except far less organized, with far less direction, help, lunch breaks, or encouragement.

I have spent the past four years desperately, anxiously waiting to get away from this place and everything it stands for only to find out, when I'm this close, that I was wrong. That I never truly would or could get away from the things I hated most about this place. In fact, it was sure to get worse.

At this point I couldn't even generate the feeling of disappointment anymore. I'm only surprised that it took my overly analytical mind this long to come to this realization but then maybe I was blinded by the hope of the possibility of something better than this. Either way, I should've known better. I should've known better than anyone that any form of appeasement for my troubles would never come as easily as a diploma.

But then this begs the question why am I here? Why am I still waiting for some light at the end of this perpetually dark and slimming tunnel? I still clung to the hope that there would be some ultimate breakthrough that would make it all worth it. I was ultimately afraid of giving up right before things started to get good, as my luck would usually have it.

And that right there was the universal answer to all my questions. I have hope.

And therefore I could still feel. I could still believe in better even if I am at my worst.

A person with hope is not a person who is prepared to give up. I have resulted that if I see things differently and I feel things differently, that I would not allow myself to not use it to my advantage. If I gave up too soon then I would never be able to see what could've been. I would never see my full potential carried out.

I have recently decided that one of my strongest features isn't that I see the bad things in the world for what they really are but that I always had hope that they could get better. Most importantly, I genuinely believe that I can change them. No matter how silly that sounded, I did, and I still want to.

That's how I knew I was far from finished.

I guess my niche isn't something obvious or common and that's what makes it special. My niche is a very small but growing group of people who think a little differently. People who don't just see bad or sad about bad, sad things, but feel such an intense reaction to it they sometimes can't handle it. But even through it all, they are still willing to change them. No matter the cost.

WHAT'S AN ADULT?

I get really bothered by the "respect your elders, respect authority," kind of people. I'm sure your learning, I get bothered by a lot of things, but these people *particularly* got all the way under my skin.

All that shit about elderly wisdom is exactly shit in my mind because I've met more than a fair amount of ignorant elders.

I get it, adulthood sucks, but adolescence isn't that much better so there's no need to blame your Sinicism on the stresses of everyday life. Everyone is stressed about life, some more than others.

For me, this is the age I'm expected to find myself, improve myself and create my future self. When I was asked to decide who I wanted to be I was still in the stage of trying to figure out who I am and to be honest I don't think I'm getting warmer.

The problem with adulthood for me isn't that I have this uncontrollable need to resist authority. My problem is that something seemed to happen to people who transitioned from adolescence to adulthood. They seemed to forget what it felt like to be stuck here, but more importantly they forgot to care.

I don't mean when your mom tells you you'll understand why she didn't let you go to that party when you have your own kids because we know damn well why she didn't right now. I mean when you look to an "elder" for help when you really need it and they basically tell you to "grow up" and "get over it."

Don't even get me started on how much I'd grown to know and hate those two pieces of "advice." I'd really like to reply to them with, "see I'd really like to but the problem is I keep having this juvenile, nagging, incessant need to either break down or disappear, but I'm sure your right. I'm sure at the exact moment I turn 18 this was all just be a laughable memory."

That being said, I'm about to be 18 and I'm still not laughing.

SELF DISCOVERY AT ITS FINEST

I reread what I write a lot just to see how fucking crazy I sounded when I wasn't in the proper state of mind.

Long story short I've noticed something really weird about the way I write.

Just as a preface, let me start by saying I usually write when I'm dead tired or generally thinking too much to handle. I'm a complete insomniac so the middle of the night, when my brain is overactive and I have nothing better to do, I find it the best time to vent write.

That means everything I write comes straight of the top of my dome so it's totally raw, honest, and unfiltered or over thought. I just free write. All my ADHD muddled thoughts somehow just file their way out onto the paper in a somewhat less confusing way. Barely, but you know I try.

Then I reread what I wrote, sometimes repeatedly, when I'm in a much better, well-rested, state of mind. It's all part of my learning about myself process.

I read all of writing multiple times before I really even noticed it, but when I did I over analyzed it like I always do.

I noticed that almost everything I write, and I mean, almost everything, is written in past tense. I have no idea why since I had wrote them right as I was thinking those thoughts or going through those things, but for some reason everything in my head had transferred over in front of me to the past tense.

Maybe it's nothing, but it's something to me. I'd written all about myself like it was a memoir, like I was already dead.

NEW BLISS

May 9 2014 12:07am

The better part of the past 17 years has been a constant series of daily mini anxiety/panic attacks on steroids. Now walking on the steps of my future college, I finally felt a feeling I had grown to believe was myth. For the first in all those years I felt calm. Despite the constant rush and chaos that is New York and college, walking on these streets of and staring at this building and these people I had finally come to know what I can only describe now as content. Hundreds of times I'd come to New York and at no time felt a feeling as elevating as this one.

In this moment I realized beyond any doubt that God was real and that all my prayers for a sign, for guidance, and for help, had been answered in this moment when the creator himself sent me this sign I had been waiting for. In this moment for the first time in what felt like forever I smiled and felt true joy that wasn't fake or forced. This is where I was meant to be. This is the path I needed to take and he was making sure that I knew that. So despite all other things that will follow or all things I'd leave behind, this is where I would start.

WORLDLY WISDOM

One of the teachings from The Analects of Confucius speaks about the importance of knowledge and what it truly means to have it. Master says, "True knowledge is to recognize when you know a thing, but also to recognize when you do not know it."

He speaks about surrounding himself with people he is certain he can learn from. He says about his companions, "there will be good qualities that I can select for imitation and bad ones that will teach me what requires correction in myself." I believe this saying to play a huge role in everyday life. I find it hugely important for everyone to recognize their flaws just as much as appreciate their attributes and that this is also a reflection of true knowledge.

I share these beliefs with Confucius because I agree with the importance of humbling yourself and surrounding yourself with uplifting, positive people who may improve on some of these flaws and who you may be able to better in return. I agree that knowledge is much more than knowing something or even knowing many things.

Like Confucius, I think critically about the quality and not quantity of the people I surround myself with. Unlike the Master I also believe that not all self-improvement should come from other people but from an individuals self experience driven by the will to expand their own knowledge.

The master also says that one important saying to consistently act upon is to "never do to others what you would not like them to do to you." Like the master, I believe that this saying is something all people should at least try to live by on a regular basis to improve everyday human interaction. It is important for people to never reciprocate negative behavior out of spite because it only generates more negative behavior. However, it is equally important for people to promote and reciprocate positive behavior in order to promote more positive behavior. Overall, I agree with most if not all of Confucius' teachings because he speaks about basic principals that all people should understand and live by, but most people don't.

STAY GOLD

4/23/14

I loved days like this. Days where I floated on a high so elevated it felt like nothing could bring me down. Sometimes I truly believed nothing ever could while others times I knew better.

In the back of mind I always felt the fear I knew all to well as the recognition that something always can. Something always seems to, no matter how hard I tried not to let it.

Even still I always chose to make the most of days like this. Even though the fear haunted and taunted me every moment, I still chose to relish in the mock untouchable happiness. It was a feeling so incredible to me that I could only understand it's intensity by recognizing that the beauty of these days -of these moments- was in their rarity like jewels and diamonds, it becomes even more precious the less often it comes around.

I thrived on these days because it was these days that reminded of what I have to look forward to. That not ALL days are bad ones and that even some can be so beautiful you actually remember them after they've long passed. Good things come and go but the really good things –the things that are worth living for- leave a permanent remnant in you. They resonate in you even when you don't know because they sometimes alter you, in small invisible ways. I'd decided that no matter how much I didn't want to live on the days that drowned me, I would always choose to live for days like this. I would always choose to let the good outweigh the bad even if it didn't seem possible because if there were still good then there would always be a reason to live. And even when there wasn't any good, the remnant of these days would allow me to push for them again.

I would always strive for days like this. That's what I've decided. If I did it for no one else or for no other reason, I would do it for myself. For days when I was untouchable and even for days when I wasn't. I would always choose to let the good days sink deep into my skin for the bad days when I needed it most and allow both to alter me because they always would, with or without my permission.

Above all things, I would choose and that was what mattered most. I would choose to control the things in my life that I could and come to terms with the things I couldn't. That was what I needed most in my life right now and I was only now realizing it, but at least I have. I could choose and I would choose. I would always choose because I could, and as long as I kept choosing, nothing else would ever be allowed to destroy me, maybe alter me, but never destroy me. At least, not without my permission.

HALF A GIRL

Oct. 1 2014 1:00am

I am in love with half of a girl.
It's hard to admit, but one half of
one girl has got me in her grip
What was once one girl has now become
a broken two because all of this girl
feels different than me and you
This girl that I love has a beautiful
smile when she glows it
A beautiful soul when she shows it
A beautiful mind but the other
half always blows it
Cause she has these beautiful lips that make
beautiful words, but that the other half
only uses to throw sharp edged swords
If you're lucky from her you'll hear a
beautiful thought if she was to share it
So beautiful you'd never know it
came from a heart of despair but also
of love that can't be compared
And this girl ... she laughs ... like a horse but
to me when she's silent, there's nothing worse

She has these perfect eyes that could see you
for things you didn't know you were.
If only she could do the same for her
I am in deep in this love with this half
that she hid cause truth be told I always
loved to play hide and seek as a kid
Each half of this girl is a half better than
my whole because without each half the
whole world seems so dull and if both her
halves never see what I see than a person
who loves in fractions is who I'll always be
A person who does love both halves of a
girl because to love one tree you must
love the whole world
So I'll just be here in love with
all she could give cause this half of
this girl needed her other half
to live.

THE GIRL WITH RED HAIR

Oct. 2 2015 2am

I had red hair for three long years.
And I'm not talking about that fake red
you can buy from a box at Sears
I'm talking about the red that was
the stuff of most parents' fears
A red that gave people the same feeling
of discomfort as when they've had too
many beers right after they're lives have
brought them right to the brink of tears
I'm talking about that you'll never get a job
at our cage with that red hair, red hair
The job that you need to bring you to the
brink of that same rage we all share
We must've got lost in translation because
we're clearly not on the same page
So let me reiterate that I do not care or I
probably wouldn't have labeled myself as
the girl with red hair
I think what shocks me the most isn't that
people react so severely to something with
a little pop

It's the fact that in comes a girl with red
hair and the whole world seems to stop
I don't want to sound dramatic, but
was it just yesterday that medicine
was considered electric shocks?
I like to believe an age of progression is where
we're living but some people make it hard
when they react more to a girl with red hair
than a human on the street shivering
This is New York and I've seen some cold
shit but I'm not talking about cold like
Let's go sit by our cozy fire pit
I'm talking about some real lack of love, which
to me is the saddest thing to see because it seems
we've all forgot that compassion is still free
This really isn't about my opinions
on trend, this is about humanity's
downward spiral to an infinite end
So let me tell you the real message
I'm trying to send;
From this point forward try to look at
every single person like they're your
best friend
If just that much help we are able to
lend then together there might still be
something here on this earth to defend
But I'm just a girl who had red hair for
a while once before you don't have to
listen to me.
This is America home of the
brave and land of the free

REAL LOVE

Oct. 2 2015 12pm

I want a real love.
That love you can't steal love.
That love that makes you really feel love
That I want that stay up all night
thinking about love, love
That stay by your side even when
push comes to shove love
That you couldn't get rid of me no
matter how hard to try love
That for you I would die love
I want love built to withstand the
end of our world kind of love
And trust me I know that's not easy to find
But lucky for me I think I still
have a fair amount of time
So as long as I'm still here I'm willing to try
(Cause truth be told I
can't do anything half way.) (2cause I
found that love and she said I don't do
anything half way) I see some
confused looks on your faces
Did I forget to say
I'm gay?

THE TRAGEDY OF MACBETH

Macbeth is a story of tragedy and despair for many reasons, but it can also be perceived as a story of good vs. evil and the unclear lines that separate them. Macbeth spends most, if not all, of the story trying to not only be king, but to maintain his hold on the crown. Meanwhile, trying to hide all of his secrets. Duncan's death is a large part of the disparity in this story and evidence that good does not always conquer evil. Despite all of Macbeth's great efforts, he too dies at the end of the story, leaving Duncan's first son Malcolm to redeem the throne. With Macbeth dead and Malcolm to redeem the throne, it leaves us wondering, what is the true meaning of *The Tragedy of Macbeth?*

The story of Macbeth starts with a king whom we don't get to see on the throne for very long. King Duncan is, as far as we know, an honest king that adores Macbeth for his many accomplishments in battle. King Duncan even names Macbeth the new thane of candor. This all adds to the suspense and despair that comes after Macbeth kills Duncan in order to usurp the throne for himself. The story between Duncan and Macbeth is a story of despair in itself. It is a story of loyalty, or lack there of. It is a reminder that no one is truly worth ALL of our trust and despite everything we may do, anyone is capable of turning on us for their own personal gain. However, it is also a story of karma as we later find out that Macbeth gets what he deserves.

The Tragedy of Macbeth was given its name for good reason: it ended in Macbeth's death. Macbeth begins the story as an honest man with nothing but honor and love for his king. Throughout the story, we witness Macbeth's downfall as he is gradually tainted by his wife and his own dark desires in a domino effect that inevitably leads to his demise. The lesson to be learned from all of this is simple: no matter what you do to excel in your own life, you will never stay on top if you don't get there honestly. Despite everything Macbeth did to obtain and hold the throne, he learned the hard way that you can't clean a mess with a dirty towel without making a bigger mess.

The story of Macbeth is indeed one of despair and tragedy. It is a story of the rises and falls of life. It is a story of the choices we make for whatever reasons and the repercussions of those decisions. Macbeth's life overall was a story of despair and even though not all the characters ended in tragedy, it is still true that they all endured it.

NOT A CHAMELEON

4/3/14

The world we live in has changed so drastically over such short time. In my mind, I imagined peaceful living, only evolving slightly over a long stretch of time. That's obviously not true because somewhere, something suddenly drastically changed everything and we've just been on a downward spiral ever since. By "something," I'm not targeting anyone or anything specific like I usually am. I mean it could've been anything from the Louisiana Purchase to the invention of the car. By downward spiral I mean that things in our world have just seemed to get worse and worse since whatever "something" happened.

Corruption is the new normal as well as isolation and with that I've realized that the depression I suffer from is just another "normal." There was a time in our history when only people who could afford it were able to see our world the way it truly was. Knowledge was power as well as it was painful. And it was expensive.

I think people who are depressed are just people who see the world for what it truly is. I truly believe that this is the truth and I also believe that's why we're so ignored. No adult wants to hear a kid tell them things they've learned to ignore. They teach you to do the same by ignoring you too.

Nowadays everyone is educated in some way. Some people just see things more critically and some people use that knowledge differently. There are people who see the truth but aren't fazed by it. They ignore it and focus on other "more important" things. Things that "are possible or reasonable." Then, there are people who see and are affected. Those people are deemed depressed. People who see sad things are saddened by them. The problem with depression is that it forces you to see all bad things and they all sadden you. It's like carrying the weight of everyone's burden on your own shoulders by yourself.

Things are becoming harder to ignore which is forcing more people to see. I think that's why more and more people are depressed now and the numbers keep growing. More and more people are saddened by the sadness that is our world. This is normal now. This is how the world is and therefore this is how the people are. Some care and some don't.

LYING IS EASY

You know when you tell a big lie and you never seem able to get away from it? Like when people keep asking questions or brining it up and you have to keep up with the lie or add to it and make the lie deeper and deeper rather than confess to all those lies together and deal with whatever that may mean?

That's what's happened to this country.

We've gotten ourselves in way too deep and now rather than confess, take the blame and begin healing the wounds, we just keep making the lies bigger and bigger till we've gotten to this place of no return.

My mom use to do this to me all the time. She'd lie or omit information (which is the same thing to me) because she thought she was protecting me from the truth. She'd face hard decisions, like divorcing my father, alone because she felt it was better to spare me the pain of knowing it was happening right next to me.

Eventually, I had to deal with the pain of the choices she made anyway. When they finally decided to divorce, I was faced with the harsh reality of the things I'd been blind to. She'd allowed me to be so ignorant so I could be happy, but I ended up both very unhappy and still ignorant.

It made it worse that she chose to hide it from me because I wasn't remotely prepared for the blow. I didn't even know to be prepared because I was never warned that I needed to be.

I don't judge any of my mom's decisions because that would crazy hypocritical. I've also become an incredible liar, but for far less noble reasons.

I literally have no idea why, but I lie about the dumbest things sometimes. My mom would ask me where I was or who I was with and even if it was the most normal, innocent thing in the world, I would still lie. I'm assuming for no other reason than to avoid further question, but still. That doesn't seem like a good enough reason to lie about random dumb shit.

For the most part, I tried to be very honest about not random dumb shit with everyone. I just feel like lying is a huge statement to your character so to me being honest wasn't just about telling the truth. Honesty means being someone people could count on and trust. I loved knowing that my – for the most part – my parents and even my friend's parents viewed me as responsible and reliable. I loved that my friends asked me questions they wanted honest answers to because they knew I would. Someone I dated once even asked if I had hung out with this person that they hated because they they this person liked me and I responded, "absolutely." That's just who I am.

It baffles me then that anyone, especially the people entrusted with running an entire country of people, wouldn't feel the same need for integrity or guilt as I do just to my parents. I simply want them to know they've raised a well-rounded girl and these people don't seem to care if anyone thinks they're good at their life's work.

I can't sleep at night feeling like I've disappointed anyone that thought better of me and they seem to sleep better, on the job, all day long, more and more.

It's all just wild to me, but hey who am I to judge, I'm broke and an insomniac.

MY MOM

I'm just really confused about what to do with my life honestly. I like to portray the girl with thick skin that's impossibly penetrated because that's the girl I was raised to be but I've learned that skin that thick is just as effective in holding everything in as it is in keeping things out. I grew up thinking emotions of any real kind were a weakness I couldn't afford so rather than leave my already weak emotional immune system even more vulnerable, I keep every thought, memory and emotion locked inside my head like a vault.

The woman that raised me is just good as good at this skill if not better, probably because she taught me.

My mom raised me in such a way that the concept of having feelings and expressing them was one I shouldn't ever even think to explore. I'm not saying my mom was a bad one, in fact I think she did exceptionally well given her circumstances - single mother, raising two young girls basically by herself. She was everything you'd expect her to be: hard working and focused. She made sure we never struggles and if we did, she made sure no one, not even me, knew about it.

She was the provider, the dad in the mom and she played all those roles very well.

I've learned so much from my mom over the years, but I've also learned so much about her. She didn't really have a father; I think that played a huge role in who she became as a grown woman. It changed me too when I kind of lost mine. Something about the absence, even if you know they're around, still effects you.

However, she never displays fear or sadness. She tries with love, but it's a difficult for her and it was something I watched her work on through the years as well. I took this trait most prominently from her.

I think she thought by saying she loved you periodically she'd done enough to remind you she did. I'm a visual learner so although I know my mother loves me; I had to look really closely to understand her ways of showing it.

Like her I have a hard time really showing this emotion. It's not like I don't want to because I really do, more than anyone knew, but it was genuinely difficult for me to display love without feeling awkward or apprehensive of the consequences it could have. I used to blame her for this problem, but I always knew it wasn't actually her fault. I thought it was genetic before I finally realized it was kinetic. I'd watched her treat emotions that way and adopted it as a great defense technique. Don't let people affect your moods, and then only you can upset yourself.

She'd also been through things she didn't know I knew. It made things make more sense for me later. It explained why she was always so afraid for me and so obsessively controlling. If she disapproved, she openly voiced it and if she could she'd change it. For the most part she avoided this problem by simply telling me how I was going to do something. *That* drove me crazy.

It isn't in my personality at all to do what I'm told, especially under the authority "because I said so." As a matter of fact, whenever possible I resisted false authority. It affects a lot of my relationships with friends, family, people I dated. Just as my issues with love and other emotions did. I always had this underlying need to control things because I hardly had control of my own life. My mother controlled my choices, school controlled my time, worrying controlled my thoughts, and I couldn't even control my own emotions. I needed to compensate somewhere, for my own sanity if we're being totally honest.

That being said, there was something about my mother I couldn't refuse.

When I was younger I used to think it was because I was scared of her. Scared of what may happen when she counted and actually reached 3. As I got older I realized fear wasn't what drove me. I obeyed my mother's most ridiculous demands, because they are demands- because I respect her. I respect the intentions behind her crazy executions because I've learned to see them for they truly are. My crazy mother was expressing her crazy version of love. She worries about me, and my sister of course, because she literally wants better for us than she had. She literally fears what could happen to us because we literally meant more to her than we knew.

So when I thought she was at her most unreasonable I would always go through the same process (after I was done bitching of course.)

First, I would probably get really mad and yell; "bitching," as I mentioned. After I remember that never works, I would find my happy place and try again with my new mindset. I would look at my mother and think about all he things we'd been through together; all the times she'd cried to me, even though there weren't that many. I would think about why she was doing what she was doing, all the reasons behind it, what she really meant when she would say "because I said so, and I'd thank her, in my head of course. She had no idea I was doing any of this so I would usually just try have a level headed adult conversation in the hopes that that could help her then see my point of you. This was 50% effective, which isn't bad if you knew my mom, hit or miss basically, but from this I learned a skill I would use for my entire life. I started viewing everything differently. I would consciously try to see things from every and all angles, preferably the positive ones. This helped me.

DEAR PASTOR BLANK

9/10/15

I touched on my relationship with my mother. I told you she was a great mom just not exactly what you expect a mom to be. That was also what would hinder me the most later. It's what brought me to this place of confusion. I'm so passionate about so many things. I've became one of those crazy people who really wants to make a difference and do something that matters because they're crazy enough to think they can, but I've also always felt like I lacked real support or guidance in my life. It discourages me to a point of just shutting down and I don't want this struggle to be the one that finally breaks me. I'm in school and I get involved in programs and things I really like so I'm making efforts to make things more positive but I've never been a big school person to begin with. The confusion is only making it harder to get the most out of this experience. The one that's suppose to be the best of my life.

I get really bad anxiety and I'm really afraid of making the wrong choices and that it will hinder me from accomplishing what I want to do for basically the rest of my life. These are the types of pressures I frequently crack under.

I've prayed on it and read and tried so many ways to stay hopeful and make paths but I feel I've exhausted them all and at this point I feel even more confused. I don't want to lose who I am in the process of trying to become who I want to become. I know this is a lot and your not a therapist but I know your really driven and clear on yourself and your goals and how to get there and I thinks that's what I really need right now.

ONLY A LITTLE SORRY

Lets not beat around the bush because I think we're very capable of differentiating fact from fiction.

You talk about protecting the people, but which people and at who else's expense? What you mean is your protecting the people you decide deserve protecting from the people you deem dangerous. Of course black and Hispanic people make up most of the population in prisons because you put them there! That isn't evidence to your claim that officers are doing their jobs. It's my entire point that they are either not doing their jobs as intended, or worse, that they are.

Regardless, the responsibility falls on someone. You could deny it or plea the fifth, but that seems to no longer even be legal these days. What would really happen if I asked any powerful official, "would you mind openly admitting that you are using your power to implement means to target particular sectors of the American population? Would you mind possibly doing so on a lie detector and I don't mean on *Maury*? No? Well that's interesting because that is exactly what you are asking of people who do not have the option of saying no because that would be plausible grounds for suspicion and would mean they have something to hide. Right …?"

"So essentially you are either saying that either your system does not work or it works so well that you yourself could fall victim to it. Does or does not refusing to answer another persons "justified" questions mean you're hiding something and if so how often? Sometimes? All the time? Then why can't you answer?"

"DRUG POLICY AS SOCIAL CONTROL"

I'm more level headed now so I'm going to calmly express my feelings about why I think this country is out to get very specific, "expendable" portions of America.

I would like nothing more than to go off about a million things from this Chomsky piece that both bothered the shit out of me and made me want to move to the U.K. However, everything I would've said, he already did and probably better than I would've.

So all I have to say is if you haven't already read "Drug Policy as Social Control," by Noam Chomsky, do so. Yesterday.

Once you have, you are more than welcome to join me in this next segment I'm calling, "1000 ways to get obliterated in America."

I read the piece mostly by my own free will. After reading it, my only thought was: how could so many people know this (or learn about it) and not be as bothered and frantic as I was.

As soon as I finished the last line – actually that's a lie. As soon as I finished the first paragraph I wanted to storm the white house, by my damn self-if I had to, and wage a war of my own.

To make matters worse, as soon as I came home and finished ranting to my father I got an answer to my first question. His only response to all this information was, "That's just the way the world is, it sucks. That's why we should all just stop watching the news and letting things make us crazy so we can be happy."

...

What?! Let me first say that I love my father to death and he's given me pretty good advice in the past. That being said, this was by far, without question, unequivocally the stupidest, most ignorant thing anyone's ever said to me. Ever.

It was also my entire point in any argument I've ever made in this general topic.

College education is at its highest in participation and promoted importance and yet everyone seems to be infected with the same viciously contagious ignorance.

Ignorance is the only way to describe it because you'd have to be a real idiot to believe that you or anyone you love is immune to the other, plentiful things trying to wipe you out.

I witnessed this very thing happen to both my parents when both they're positions were "terminated" in two very different fields.

Granted my father lost his job, and much more years before the same problem touched my mother but the point remains exactly the same. No one is safe. Not the high school dropout, *DHL* delivery truck driver of over 14 years college or the college graduate, *CNN* executive assistant of over 20.

Not you.

Not me.

There is a structure in place, designed to preserve a small "minority" and exterminate a much larger one. That's kind of the problem. You did not design this structure - though you do play a significant role in its survival – and therefore does not consider you or your needs in the slightest.

To put things into perspective: if the world were ending and there were only 5 life boats all separated by hierarchy, you still wouldn't be on any of them.

People have become so disgustingly comfortable and I'm just trying to figure out what about any of this is comforting. I'll speak for myself when I say I know I definitely don't sleep soundly knowing that the system that is suppose to protect and therefore has been placed above me, is up planning my demise, outwardly or not.

Its apparent that practically no one will ever feel a need to acknowledge and/or change anything unless they themselves are at they're lowest point, feeling its terror firsthand.

Of course, by then it would be far too late for them to even hope to send a message to anyone because they would be nothing more than another casualty of the war on the weak.

They would be the sad faces we ignore on the street and in the subways and one day they could very well be us, our faces.

THE SUPERHERO MYTH

I've always found the "human ideal" as a whole to be an interesting social norm placed on everyone by no real source.

We are all just expected to be a version of human that quite frankly doesn't even exist and if it does it is entirely too small of a minority to be setting the bar for everyone else. Still, each gender is assigned its own expectations considered to be essential components to this genders ideal of success and what's most baffling is that each genders expectations are a complete contrast to the other because it is the opposite gender setting that standard. Gomez refers to a mans emotions as an "embarrassment," to his "journey to becoming a man (Gomez 1). Men are taught from childhood that ordinary men who, "were striving to grow and learn and ask questions and risk being wrong and be humble ... (Gomez 2)", really had no place in this world. Men are raised to idolize other men who are successful businessmen or all star athletes, while women are raised to idolize and chase Photoshop beauty. As Gomez points out in his own childhood memory, boys are encouraged to participate in activities that would earn them scholarship opportunities while women are encouraged to be obsessive of they're appearance whether or not they're fashion forward shoes ever step on a college campus. What's worse is that we all then wonder why we've raised such arrogant prehistoric men *and* women. The important concept here is not whether men or women struggle more hardships in today's society. The significant concept is why it is anyone is expected to fit into a "gender role" and why, knowing that it is not only wrong but also impossible, we still find ourselves trying to fit into them.

This concept is extremely important to Gomez's point because it expresses the mistreat of all genders in todays society. By, claiming that men are also suffocated under the pressures of "being a man," he introduces the idea of unity between both sexes to work to end this means of oppression and loss of self. Rather than attack each other, men and women should work together to encourage individuality. Humans together must realize that the key to becoming the most successful person you can be is not to chase a fairy tale that does not really exist but by being *yourself* because that is the only thing you can perfectly be. "It took me recognizing the messy, beautiful, human complexity inherent in this life, to finally realize that I could be a "good man" without having to be Superman or the Perfect Man … Supermen do not exist (Gomez 2)"

A WOMEN'S BEAUTY?

The relationship between women and their bodies seems to be stronger than ever in this generation and this country. I don't mean women and girls are becoming more comfortable with their bodies, I mean they're learning to be more comfortable with how to use them. Females are encouraged more now to worry more about what their bodies look like and therefore are worth, than what those bodies are doing. Susan Sontag rightfully states in her essay of women's beauty, that this birth responsibility often outshines any other accomplishment in a women's life. Women who are considered "beautiful" seem to already have an advantage in life over "average" women despite all other variables.

I'm not going to name names but lets imagine a publicly known and generally accepted group of people who happen to be family and happen to have found the limelight through one family members interesting ability to make X-rated home movies and an inhumane ability to control the transfer of her body fat. This would also be an entire family that has collectively built and maintained an entire career based on essentially looks alone. I guess you cold call it strong understanding on how to work a system or you could also call it having enough money to alter it. Also imagine that that same family member from earlier goes on to take paid jobs that required her to pose nude after she has already expressed a level of remorse for her previous X-rated movie? Oh and she's also had a child, a girl. What would bother me most her choice of self-expression but her defense, that this choice is an expression of love for her body. Should women really live up to what is expected or desired of them in order to be free? Or is love for your body really expressed through it being publicly displayed? There truly may be no right or wrong answer, but for the little girl who will learn under those morals will never know another way.

THE POWER OF SEX

<hr />

Would you understand me if I said I never understood how people were capable, and allowed, to question one another, but never question why it is we question each other. As human beings we have all been blessed with the ability to form our own opinions and as Americans to express them. Yet so often we choose not to. So often we choose to believe and enforce the opinions of anyone but ourselves, under the pretense that these opinions *are* our own. I've always found humanity as a whole to be interesting. Interesting that though genetically built 90% the same, together we have found enough wiggle room in that other 10% to create a Grand Canyon sized gap between each other, as well as whom we are or are truly supposed to be. We are each expected to be a version of something that, quite frankly, doesn't even exist and if it does is entirely too small of a minority to be setting the bar for everyone else. Still, each sex is assigned its own expectations considered to be essential components to its definition of success. What's most interesting is that nowhere in these expectations is there any room for insertion of a gray area. Both sexes are consistently in complete contrast to each other because if women are to be weak than a man must be strong. Women are meant to be invested in their appearance while men are meant to be invested in … themselves. There is power in sex, but like all great powers, there must be a power to control it.

Who is a real woman? How does she look, dress, talk, or act? What is she interested in or do in her spare time? If you look at pretty much any publicized woman you are more than likely only going to get the wrong answers. Despite what any magazine would tell you, most women actively living in the 21st century do not naturally think about every poor on their face all day long. Don't get me wrong; chances are if you ask any random woman about her biggest insecurities, she's not going to say not knowing more about politics. What she will say more than likely will have something to do with how she looks. I'm guilty of it as I'm sure most women are. But can we be blamed? This is what we've been taught to make a priority our entire lives because as ridiculous as it sounds, a woman's appearance is her biggest tool in success. If you read the job requirements for most women in high social standing you will find somewhere in the ladder that she had to be someone she wasn't. For women any involvement beyond a superficial one is an effort wasted. So why then must a woman decide that in order to feel fulfilled in her life she must emanate sex she will later be judged for? At the end of the day this is a choice that women are *deciding* to make, not that they have many other options. There is a reason every time you turn on a TV or look at an ad; you are faced with a half naked woman or women who are genetically impossible. Simply: sex sells, women are viewed as sex and women are selling themselves. Is this really a women's power or because it seems like women are grasping for a power for someone else's use. "Women *are* the beautiful sex-to the detriment of the notion of beauty as well as of women (Sontag 118) ... beauty is power ... it is the only form of power that women are encouraged to seek ... If a women does real work, she brings under suspicion her very capacity to be objective, professional, authoritative, thoughtful" (Sontag 119). The sad truth is that if more products were advertised staring an average looking woman, average looking women would be much less interested. "Average" is now a standard considered below average, because woman have allowed themselves to be convinced that they themselves are not good enough for themselves.

What does it mean to be a real man? Unfortunately, I personally can't tell you myself. What I can tell you is why I think men are shaping our world with clay already hardened. From childhood men are raised to believe that men who, "were striving to grow and learn and ask questions and risk being wrong and be humble ..." (Gomez 2), really had no place in this world. What if those gender "roles" were reversed? According to Sara Boboltz of *The Huffington Post*, if you looked into some points in history you would find that they were. In the 1600s it was perfectly normal, even practical for men to wear high heels. What started as a necessity when riding horseback evolved into a common part of men's fashion and masculinity. Lace fabrics were viewed similarly during the same time but, unlike man heels, lacked any practical origin besides one of fashion. Would you believe me if I said cheerleading started as a man's sport? Being a cheerleader was viewed as one of the manliest accomplishments a man could take away from college before the 1920s because it was viewed too "masculine" for women. If anyone told a man today it was essential to his manhood to bring back these trends, should or *would* he simply adjust without further question? Those who claim they have drawn a line they wouldn't cross, are lying. The fact is it doesn't really matter what we're being told, as long it's said in a way we'll respond well too. Clearly it wouldn't be a crazy concept to imagine that if "society" really wanted things to be this way again or any way at all, they could and we would instinctively oblige. What a struggle it would be for today's man to adapt to a world where they were judged on appearance, but if it did happen, we'd all see a lot more men in heels.

Men are raised to idolize and strive to be other men who embody all different types of ultimate success, while women are raised to idolize and chase a Photoshop beauty and view this beauty *as* success. As children boys are encouraged to be involved in activities that would earn them scholarship opportunities while girls are encouraged to be consumed to the point of obsession with their appearance whether or not they're fashion forward shoes ever step on a college campus. We then all have the nerve to wonder why we've continued to raise generations of ignorant, prehistoric men *and* women. "It took me recognizing the messy, beautiful, human complexity inherent in this life, to finally realize that I could be a "good man" without having to be Superman or the Perfect Man … Supermen do not exist" (Gomez 2). We are mankind and what matters is not whether men or women's lives are more imposed on more by society. What matters is why it is anyone is expected to fit into any role and why, knowing that it is not only wrong, but impossible, we still find ourselves dying to fit into them.

Who really decides what role a women or a man should play in our society? Some would say men and some would say other women. Regardless, when did people adopt such an extreme need for outside approval? A woman should decide the dynamic of the relationship with herself and with the rest of the world, just as a man should. This is the only true power that anyone has from birth until death: the power of yourself. No other power or person should or could take this decision from anyone without permission. This is not to say that your own choices will always be easy or accepted but at the very least, they will be *your own*. Meanwhile, hidden in the background of this endless struggle, lies a question some of us will go the rest of our lives without ever asking. Who am I? If you're too busy trying to be someone else, how could you ever really know?

NEW YEAR'S EVE

11/28/14

New Year's is my favorite holiday. It sounds overly sentimental, but I literally always cry. Anyone who knows me knows that it must be a national holiday for you to catch me crying and even then I'd do anything in my power to act like I'm not.

My family treats it like a red carpet event so coming from where I come from, this is the only day a year, or in my life, that I can get all over dressed.

Every member of my big ass Spanish family would all gather in the living room and watch the ball drop together, or rather, yell the countdown together and before we even got to say Happy New Year, I'd be crying.

I really don't know what it is. Of course it has something to do with the idea of putting a whole year behind me and starting a whole new one, but I know it's so much more than that for me. It's like knowing I got through another year and I can get through another one. It has a lot to do with looking around and being in the same room with the same people every year that I love. It's the only holiday my parents are in the same building and we all get to experience that moment together. This day means more to me than any holiday, birthday, or special event I get all year long.

It's about to be another New Year and now I guess is the time for reflection. In 2014, I changed a lot, but so much has.

China became the world's largest economy, which isn't surprising since they pretty much own us. It just says a lot about where we're heading. America was always considered a world power, but when you really get into it, we really ain't shit. China could take us at any moment and there's really nothing we could do about it. For all we know, 2015 could be the year they do it.

We also went back to war with Iraq, which to be honest, bothered me more than a lot of events of 2014 and more than it did most people. I liked Obama so much during his election because he didn't support our involvement in other countries problems, much less to the point of going to war. Our national debt is way too high for us to be spending most of our annual national budget on wars that aren't ours. This year, we forgot that again.

EVERY SINGLE TIME

Sep. 15 2015 1:10am

You know when you're on antibiotics and your doctor tells you to finish the whole prescription even if you start to feel better? That's what this feels like to me. Every single time.

It's like someone or something happens that starts to make me feel better for a little while and just when I start to get comfortable in this and think everything is finally better, the infection slowly creeps back in and completely infects me. If I thought

I usually just quarantine myself and try to figure out what my next move is like I'm playing a game of strategy with myself. Every single time. Every time I think I've finally kicked it, it kicks me again.

I was becoming more and more understanding of why some cancer patients choose to stop treatments. You keep fighting and fighting only to find your body keeps betraying you.

How many times can one person take that instability in one lifetime before they finally crack? I guess I was finally finding out why some people don't make the whole lifetime.

"THE ALLEGORY OF THE CAVE"

My teacher was lecturing about "The Allegory of the Cave" today in my English class. She spoke about humans being imprisoned in their own minds and by the world. She asked us, "How someone who has imprisoned their entire life would even know they're imprisoned."

A girl I recognized as one of the more intellectual thinkers in the class answered with, "when they are told the truth of their imprisonment." My teacher replied, "But what is the truth? Who is to say that the man wasn't truly imprisoned when he was taken out of the cave? Who is to decide that when you are taken out of one ignorance you aren't just as bound if not more?"

If you've never read "The Allegory of the Cave", it's basically a short story about a man who is taken from always being chained on a chair to see the outside world. He is taught to see objects for they *really* were in the hopes that he would one day be able to see and except them as such so one day he may even look upon the sun itself. I felt for the guy, I really did. I could only imagine how difficult it would be for me if someone told me that everything I've ever known was a lie. It was hard enough the first time.

Wait, you thought this was an analogy? It's a reality we've all learned to ignore. At some point in our lives someone or something has dragged us all out of our cave and forced us to learn to look at the sun. I'm not talking about when someone told you that Santa Clause wasn't real. I'm talking about when you learned that the animals you loved at the petting zoo were the same ones being slaughtered so you could have a hamburger at a pool party. I'm talking about when you made the conscience choice to ignore that fact so you wouldn't have to feel guilty about loving said hamburger.

I love hamburgers, so I'm in no way saying you should stop enjoying them, but the fact is for every hamburger you choose to enjoy, a cow must've died, literally and metaphorically.

As the class debated about a topic I was more than interested in, I sat quietly thinking about this story couldn't be a better personification of the things I thought about on a regular basis. Who decides things are what they are said to be? Who decides that these decisions are worthy of following? Why do we follow? This class had done more to give me questions then answer them. I'd also come to recognize that this was the point of the entire class. This woman appeared in the path of our lives so we could people who asked questions, not blindly follow. A person that is hard to find among people now.

I have reaaal problems with the idea of formal education as a whole. I firmly believe that Malcolm X probably provided himself with a better education in a prison cell, than most people receive throughout their entire lives and thousands of dollars. I believe that forcing KIDS when we know they're at their most impressionable to go to "schools", is not a way of improving people, but a way of making money while installing the microchip necessary for their future oppression.

I firmly believe that this the reason I never did well in school … okay maybe I just didn't test well, but that's probably because I wasn't made to be tested to someone else's standard. Yet here I am. In a college classroom. The *only* means of "education" that I could've actually opted out of by "choice." I could've very easily decided not to come here but would it really have been possible to succeed without it?

I know people like to make the "Steve Jobs succeeded without a college degree" reference and he wouldn't be the only one. Tons of people have made careers on their own accord and my father is himself among them. Still even my father has always pushed me into going to college and I have always assured him I would because me and my father both know just as you do, that my chances for success without it would be microscopic. That Steve Jobs is dead and with him I think also died those possibilities.

If there ever was another road to success, I'm more than sure it was just a crack in a carefully constructed system thought to be unbreakable because it was believed we'd never find it. So sad that so many think so little of the underdogs of the world because to their amazement, we did find it, some of us at least.

Unfortunately, they realized we did just as quickly and the crack was sealed better than the walls that surrounded the Glade of The Maze Runner. The problem is we hadn't yet found the way out. We came dangerously close and threatened by the possibilities of what "freedom" truly looked like, we ran back into the glade before we could find out. Believing that the dangers within were less frightening than the dangers outside we allowed ourselves to believe when we were told there was no way out even if we wanted it and that looking would be dangerous. We settled with the idea that this just wasn't our time and we should instead continue to send our runners to search and report back when it was clear and safe, assuming they ever would.

It has never been and will never be clear and safe. There are few runners but they know things they want to share with us so that we may run farther together. King, Malcolm, Lincoln, Kennedy, *they* were the runners we were waiting to lead us to freedom and we have chosen to ignore their maps. They are telling us what paths are safest and how to navigate them but we must choose to run it ourselves despite others disapproval. There *is* a way out that can only be found when the sun has set and we have seen the other stars: their shapes and their sizes. I choose everyday to try to look past the sun because I have a different idea of knowledge and they're not teaching it here.

The fact is someone must drag you out of your cave but you must choose whether or not you want to look directly at the sun and once you do you must also choose how you view and utilize the light. The sun is one start in a sky full of them. Of course it's the biggest and shines the brightest, but that does not make it anymore immune to explosion than any other star. I would argue that a sky full of stars is far more beautiful than one that covers the rest. As a matter of fact, no other star will hurt your eyes or cause as much damage as looking just at the sun. The trick is waiting for the sun to reach its set and finding all the stars as they take their opportunity to rise.

FOOD FIGHTS BACK

Food is supposed to be essential to survival. I think we've taken it to an ultimate extreme, but it's still true. I think it's kind of scary that people are more aware than ever of how horrible some of the stuff they put in their bodies is and that they still choose to eat it.

To add my already abnormally high anxiety, I also just learned that the Health Administration announced that all forms of meat cause cancer. Perfect.

I was a vegetarian once when I saw a documentary about how animals are slaughtered. It made me feel so horrible about eating them and overall being a human. I was only really a vegetarian for a maybe five months before I realized I couldn't do it. Instead I settled for not eating red meats, which I stick to till this day but that's beside the point.

Now we're finding out that *all* meats could kill us just as gruesomely. I used to feel bad that we were killing these animals – I still do – but now I know they're also killing us.

The "weaker" minorities found a way to fight back, good for them.

McDonalds is probably just as likely to kill you as smoking on a regular basis, but I have yet to see a "Dare to keep Children off diabetes," program. In fact your "happy meals" now include a cute toy to distract you and your young ones from your high blood pressure.

I hate McDonalds more than I hate math equations and I *despise* math but I'd be lying straight out of my ass if I told you I didn't occasionally enjoy some Wendy's or certain other infamous names. In my defense, it's not even like I always have a choice considering these days, it's harder to find foods that will extend and improve your quality of life than foods that will do the opposite. It's also 5 times more expensive.

So only the wealthy can really eat healthy? That's insane. Just another crazy way for the rich to own the world considering everyone else will be too busy dying prematurely to do anything about it.

DRAMATIC IRONY

Oct. 29 2015

We aren't and have never been the minority
Haven't you realized that's just they're poorly
   supported story
They're directors of organized chaos
In charge of keeping you chasing the mirage
So you never think to look past they're poorly
   constructed facades
Keep your friends close and your enemies under
   control
That way they'll never try to change any of your
   roles
We are stronger in groups and they know it that's
   what has them so scared
It's just never been done because until now no one
   dared
What would you really do if all those "minorities"
   you thought you'd handled together decided to
   finally fight back?
What could you do if they realized they could
   exterminate you too, just like an overambitious
   gnat?

Get rid of your whole hierarchy but then who will
    you control?
They'll be nothing and no one left to forfeit the
    things you already stole
The roles are being changed I'm sorry to say, you'll
    no longer be in a place of authority
Because in both our hierarchies, we were and are
    still the majority

EVERY MAN FOR HIMSELF

2/6/15

I am deadly afraid of airplanes. I'm probably being grossly over dramatic when I say deadly, but I know I'm not the only one who has light heart convulsions when the second I step onto an airplane.

I don't think it helps either when they start playing that damn safety video. I recognize that it's suppose to be for our safety of course, but when you take an already incredibly scary situation and add to that an incredibly paranoid teenager, it just doesn't seem smart to begin by pointing out all the horrible things that could possibly go wrong.

The ironic part about this whole thing is that the video actually kind of helps me a little in some way. Not for actual safety reasons because lets be honest, "in the event of an emergency," I would probably just panic, forget all those instructions, and die of self induced heart attack.

It helped me because every time it played, I would always get stuck on this one part that I would replay over and over again in my head and would usually distract m for hours.

It was the part about air pressure or oxygen, or something like that the cabin. It's the part that they show you the facemasks dropping from the ceiling and they give you instructions on what to do if this happens. This part always caught my attention because this is the part where the same annoying host lady would say that you should fasten your mask on your face before helping anyone else. Every time I watched it, they would show a women putting on her mask before putting it on a child sitting next to her. You have no idea what the relationship was between the two people. All you know is that for some reason they felt a need to make it clear no matter who is around you, you should put on your own mask before anyone else and that is exactly the women in the video was doing.

That right there scared me more than the obviously very scary threat of loss of oxygen. Every time I saw this part of the video, I was reminded of where I come from. I couldn't and still can't rap my head around a world where we can and are openly saying to save yourself before anyone else. Nonetheless, find it normal.

Every time I got on a plane and saw this part, I would usually go off on a mental tangent about all the things in our world that paralleled this value. The values that we should each consider ourselves more valuable than anyone and everyone around us in order to survive. Whether or not we are worth saving, we shouldn't be concerned. Survival is all that matters? That seems like a horrible way to live, but it is our way of life.

I have no problem admitting that I am in no way a perfect saint, but it is for that reason that if one of the wings on this plane blows up right now, I literally couldn't see myself putting myself before anyone on a scale of importance, especially a small child.

If I've learned anything in my short life it's that people are just like planes. We are incredible products of science and technology that require thousands if not millions of components to function properly. But when functioning properly, we can be the vessel for incredible, world-altering exploration. If just one of all those parts is missing or slightly off, we can just as easily be the cause of horrible disaster.

Just like planes, people function similarly.

We are all made of someone else's parts and none of us would be who we are without having first taken something from someone else. What an incredible thing it would be if everyone moved through the world and their lives with this thought at the front of their minds. If we all reminded ourselves that everything we throw out in the world may never find its way back to us but will more than likely be picked up by someone else.

I think about how different everyone would be in a world like this all the time. Not just that the air would be more breathable, but that more people would be happier, more appreciative to breathe it. I wonder how people would want to bring children into a, "fasten your face mask on your face before helping anyone else," kind of world.

And then I wonder how I could possibly be the only person who thinks about this.

WE'RE DOOMED

I learned about Denver International Airport today, from *YouTube*. I agree it's probably not the most credible source, but I would argue the facts in it are undeniable. If you've never heard of it, I highly suggest you look it up; it's worth your time.

The whole idea centers on the conspiracies of "The New World Order." I get most of this stuff is based on exactly that, conspiracy, but if you really took the time out to do some research on the things you normally wouldn't question or maybe you do but ignore, you would find some questionable things at least.

I'm not going to go into depth about every last scary detail about the airport so I'll just give you the summarized version and leave the rest up to the Internet.

Basically, people believe the airport is going to be used as a concentration camp during the creation of a new world due to the random empty buildings buried under the airport that keep being secretly worked on. Apparently Denver already had a functional airport and didn't need a new one that is pretty much the same except that it has fewer tracks than the old one and is built in the shape of a swastika. The plaque in the airport that credits its creation to something called the, "New World Commission," is crediting a group that doesn't exist. All the creepy artwork of dead children and doves by giant green soldiers in gas masks doesn't really help either.

After watching the videos, I will shamelessly admit that it raised questions for me. Why were the buildings buried? If they were considered mistakes, then why do they continue to work on them and deny it rather than demolish like they usually do? Why those murals and what do they represent? When anyone is asked any questions about the airport, they receive no answers. That in itself raises huge questions. The biggest: if there's nothing to hide, why not put an end to the rumors?

I swear I'm usually not so easily convinced on these types of things. I'm a realist so even though I absolutely believe there's some sneaky shit going on under our noses; it would take a lot to convince me that I should be afraid of an airport.

That being said, the airport isn't what ended up scaring me at all. It's the slap in the face that it represents.

A mural like that absolutely has a message and it's not a beautiful story of rebirth. You'd be lying to yourself if you said it was.

It's a message that has been placed right in front of you to do nothing about.

Whoever is in charge of this new world, is so confident in themselves and their success that they are literally painting you a picture of what's going to happen.

They are unafraid of people like you and I. They think they're untouchable.

This is just one example of the things that your not only being hidden from but that you're choosing to bypass. You could call any one person crazy but if you actually took the time to go on your smartphone and lookup just one question you had you'd find the answers you didn't want to hear.

Enough people are asking those same questions and giving you enough similar answers to believe there may be some level of truth behind it. We're talking people with college degrees just as much as people with too much time on their hands. You could know just as much about the scary facts as they do if you wanted to.

The real facts you actually have to look for the things you should know about because they are not going to willingly share it with you. Your sources are only going to tell you what random thing Miley Cyrus is doing and what Nicki Minaj is wearing.

EDUCATION EVOLUTION

Nov.2 2015

My mythology teacher is high school admitted to me that the system in place in schools doesn't really allow teachers to be teachers anymore. They could obviously teach, but basically only what they were told or permitted to teach about. She said she would propose new ideas to her authority and they would knock them down as being unfit or unimportant.

Essentially she told me the entire point of teaching, as a teacher was a myth in itself, but not one she was allowed to teach about.

When you really think about what that means, it's a far bigger issue on a far bigger scale than it sucking to be a teacher these days. It's an issue that involves social training this early in our lives.

You are willingly sending your kids to institutions where teachers can't teach. This way what they actually learn is that asking question, as well as finding and/or sharing answers is dangerous, and conformity is vital. You are learning that you should separate yourself from people unlike you, but you should not talk about too much with people who are. Any derailment from this system could mean disaster, but for who?

If you believe this to be a proper form of education, than that exact education system has done its job on you flawlessly.

This is meant to be the land of freedom and opportunity for a reason. The problem is, none of us are demanding either one.

In high school, I learned that high school isn't suppose to teach you anything that will make you one of the 3% that possess 70% of the money in this country. In fact, it's quite the opposite if you ask me. It teaches you how to be more "comfortable" in the remaining 97% fighting for the hidden and heavily guarded 30% of remaining money. It teaches you that even if you do come out on top, you should sit in your wealth with quiet gratitude and let the system that allowed you sit there, continue to do what it does or your seat can be replaced.

In high school, I learned that being in the stage of adolescence is where you set the stage for your entire life. Not just because your required to decide your college and your major, but because this is the place where the young people of the world are taught to look away from the things we should be looking at and focus our attention elsewhere. It's where you are taught your ole and how exactly you can play it safely.

Very few are able to notice that or want to, but the ones who do are the people who choose to look the other way.

College is something very different for me.

In college, they understood all those things or at least I got lucky enough that my teachers did. In college, teachers could teach about whatever they wanted to, I guess. I credited this with being the reason my first college level class taught me more than I'd ever really learned in my life.

Not to say I've never learned anything, but my college English class taught me more things of value than, I can honestly say, ever before.

I learned more things that actually made me question other things around me as well as within me.

I was no longer comfortable living under the means I'd been living and I couldn't understand for the life of me how anyone else could be.

It physically pained me to watch anyone, especially those close to me, live passably.

I hate to see people struggle. I hate even more to see other people over look people who are struggling.

I've never had the born talent they say most New Yorkers seem to have that allows them to walk by a person lying on the street and not even flinch. I bought more over priced New York hotdogs for those people than I ever bought for myself.

It was never a matter of being recognized or making myself feel like an angel of God.

It was about being a person that other people would ridicule you for being or that they firmly believed didn't exist.

I am far from perfect but I refuse to believe that what we have made of this world is all it or we are capable of. I do believe that it has stopped advancing and definitely begun digressing, but only because we have allowed it to. Of course at some point we have to accept the blame for our own demise. We can't simply lay down and watch someone try to murder us and complain that we were killed because no one came to save us, that no one taught us self defense, or that they're weapons were stronger. Any of those answers would be irrelevant, untrue, or an excuse.

If you are ok with living a mediocre life and living everyday hoping that the little you have doesn't slip through your frail fingers than by all means continue to do just that and close this book immediately, it will scare you.

If you have miraculously achieved some level of success and firmly believe that, that position is so solidified in your life that it could never be taken from you either than, your wrong, but you too should continue to shield your eyes.

If you stay up at night thinking about the many things that have infected and corrupted the world you live in, that this is the world that your allowing to thrive for your children, and that you need to do something before you really can't, than you and I, are thinking the same thing.

I am 18 years old and I am haunted daily by the road that we are going down. I am petrified that no one will ever decide it's time to stop playing stupid and save us.

I will not allow my children to grow up in this world or the world that it is surely becoming. Even If I die trying I will do anything in my power to be that savior that everyone else seems to be waiting for.

Maybe you have no children and you think that none of this is problem because your troubles end when they bury you.

If your one of those people I genuinely hope, with everything in my heart, I mean this, that you are reincarnated right back where you started so you do indeed get to witness firsthand the shit show you allowed to happen.

We are living a real life hunger games and, both our biggest problems are originating from the Capitol.

You really think these things are coming from the creativity of people's minds? People are surely creative, but let's be realistic for once.

Writers like Gary Ross, James Dashner, and Kass Morgan were inspired by examples very close to home.

Unlike these writers, I refuse to use some fantastic story to make you begin to see things for what they truly are.

I refuse to baby the people of this country anymore than they already have been by succumbing to everyone's need to have everything completely coated in sugar in order for them to swallow it.

Nov. 3 2015

I've come to learn a lot about my English teacher. Like I think she may be part of a small revolution aiming toward the savior of our world.

She talks about a lot of the same things I think about and she thinks about them a lot of the same way I do.

She talks about the corruption of our system, the end of the world as we know it, and where it'll all leave us in the end. She also talks about all the other people who are also thinking these things. People I other wise have never and probably would never have heard about. She does it all in such a way that makes her seem unbiased but I think she feels exactly how I do. I think she won't openly say it because she wants us to draw our own conclusions and decide our own level of interest. She wants us all to stop playing stupid like every other generation seems to have done and do something actually different. Not the different that the media will convince you to be, but actually different. I didn't even know an English class could be about these things but then part of me things it's not. I think she's choosing to be a different kind of teacher in hopes that she'll create a different kind of adult. An adult that cares enough to do things everyone else is too afraid or too preoccupied to be.

I appreciate all those things about her. We need more people like her. People who are contributing even in a small way to bring to light and solve the problems that will inevitably end us.

She gives me hope that my hyperactive feelings and efforts aren't wasted. That those people are actually out there, they're scattered and really hard to find.

This is good news because this is the base that we can build our new world on. This is what we've been lacking and the only reason their world has evolved so much better than ours. A small group that is organized and clear in their intent is naturally going to get farther than billions of angry people who have separated themselves from their only potential allies.

To be a strong competitor you must think both like yourself and your opponent. Have clear, organized plans and have strong allies to back you up.

This is what they've tried to prevent because it is the best and only road to real victory.

I'm seeing more and more real, positive change and we need to keep this cycle going.

We must start to think more like our opponent: be tactical, smart but strong in our planning, and quiet. That way, just like they thought they'd do to us, they'll never see us coming and they'll be surprised but what we've brought.

Nov. 2 2015

I want to live in a world that is completely different
    than whatever world I'm living in now
You call this home but I call this survival of the
    fittest on open hunting grounds
How can anyone sleep soundly when literally
    nothing in your life is guaranteed?
You could lose anything and everything at any
    moment, even the things you don't have yet,
    even the air you breath
You could say I'm dreaming big but I want to live
    in world that doesn't make me scared, kind of
    nervous, pretty much anything but free
A world where I can be me and succeed and not
    have to constantly watch my back for whoever
    or whatever is trying to kill me

"LISTEN TO THE KIDS"

"Listen to the Kids." Some wisest words I've ever heard and they came from, Kanye West.

I think about those words regularly and not because they're one of few words I understood from the speech they were from, but because they were the wisest words I'd ever heard any person in a position of power say and it was a *rapper.*

I'm not sure if he meant it the way I took it, but through whatever message he was trying to send all I really heard was, "listen to the children."

He was right. We should be listened to.

We should be listened to because we have served our time of listening and now have something to say. We have gathered enough information to know how to say it.

MY TIME CAPSULE

24 minutes of empty

10:00 am
I felt weak weakness
not a feeling but an emotion
no attention
no forgiveness
I felt it all through out my veins
it started with in my wrists then went all the way
up my arms
now there's chills
when the winning banner is cut down the middle,
it's just a ribbon.
weakness
not a feeling
but an emotion.

10:05 am
I felt empty
5 minutes prior I felt everything
now there's nothing.
I found myself crying 5 minutes ago
now there's not a care in the world

my body and mind is defined as inconclusive at this very moment.
what are feelings? I want to know. of course I have them, but why do they have an effect on me, even when I'm empty inside? I just don't get it.

It's 10:15 and I'm tearing
there's many reasons to cry in my life
but I don't like to cry
crying overcomes my fake happiness
my happiness isn't real but I hope one day it will be
my heart is full of love, equality, and forgiveness.
I have people that "love" me, I'm living life ... that's enough to be fake happy for right?
stay bright, breathe, just keep smiling.

My cheeks remain moist from my tears about 10 minutes ago, but it's 10:24 and now I'm full of questions.
my head won't stop pounding with them.
At the moment love seems to be the thing I'm most questionable about.
My precedent self wouldn't let anything worth loving approach her, the old me slipped away and now I'm here.
The thing I despise the most about love is that you can't trust it. Love builds up all the insecurities you have and enchases them by a thousand.
When I'm laying next to him and he hugs me from behind ... I feel secure, its the best feeling ever.
when he lets go for even a second I feel my insecurities come up once more. For that long second I feel distrust, negativity, sadness, and lies lots and lots of lies

the worst thing is it's probably me, it's all in my
head. But I just can't help it.
I guess that's love right?
2 seconds go by and he hugs me again,
no more weakness, questions, and no insecurities.
everything's okay now.

- Jackie, 18

My life isn't "cool." I'm not broken, there's nothing
wrong with me. I just view things differently
from all the experiences I've been through. I'm
selfish. I think about my feelings and my needs
and whoever gets in the way is bound to get hurt.
I apologize to all those who hurt me or have been
hurt by me. I'm just a child. Is that bad?

My time is coming soon if it's just me crossing
the street and getting hit by a car or even me
taking my own life. It's a sin and illegal to kill
yourself because that's the only real control you
have in this life.

What if we wake up and all of this was made
up? They say God gives the strongest soldiers the
worst problems, but no soldier of God. I'm a fallen
angel, ready to get off this ever-lasting world.

- Nick, 16

The world around us can feel like a hectic place,
but it's how you respond as a person to the
craziness that defines you. It's difficult to live in
it, but overall, it has shaped me to become who
I am today. The world throws challenges at me

non-stop, causing me to feel like giving up is the only way out.

It's just a shame that a world as amazing as ours can make each and every human, at a point, come to an end.

As a person, I believe that the struggles you face throughout your life, shape you into the person you become. In my eyes, I've always viewed the world as a nightmare that I wanted to escape but I couldn't. Growing up, I never knew what happiness felt like.

I never knew what it felt like to be fully content with my life.

Everyday, I would look in the mirror and feel everything but beautiful. Putting a smile on my face and acting like everything was okay was the only way to hide these feelings and the only way I would avoid other people asking me about them.

At night, nothing but negative thoughts would run through my mind. I would cry myself to sleep at night wondering why I could never be as happy as all my friends and why I could never make anybody happy. The stress of pain, unhappiness, and fears of unachieved goals, fueled my desire to end it all but I always had a piece of me that just could not give up. I always felt that everybody that walked into my life would hurt me because that was all I was used to.

I always make sure that the people I love are happy and do whatever it takes for them to feel the way I always wanted somebody to make me feel.

The world can be a bruising place for some people. If the world did not lack so much positivity and happiness, it would be easier to live in. But *we live in a world where speaking on your feelings will cause others to judge you or make you feel abnormal, so most of us just bottle all of our emotions, which causes us to feel this way.*

- Anonymous, 18

Growing up in a loveless society, I've always felt like an extreme outcast. No matter how hard I tried, I just couldn't fit in. Eventually, that led me to believe that something was wrong with me. Many past relationships of mines just seem to add onto that problem, leaving me with more questions than answers such as, was I too kind? Did I say the wrong thing? Did I love too much? I began to think that love was my weakness. It wasn't until I found out that there were other's like me, did I begin to finally appreciate myself for who I was, "A Hopeless Romantic!" I want love, I dream of it, and still have hope that I will find my one true love, although society says otherwise. It's just in my nature.

"We Found Love"

We found love in hopeless shares
Of our bodies,
After being broken for so long,
Continuously tormenting ourselves,
For ever lending our souls out in the first place.
We found love,
Which soon led to our minds,
Once we broke the chains

Of emotional confinement,
And learned to love again.
But after being broken for so long
After the one too many heartbreaks,
After you were told to hide your love,
After you were told you cannot be loved,
After society declared romance dead,
So did you.
Slowly but surely ...

Slowly but surely,
you learned to hide it,
and become like the rest,
Thinking it will solve your problems.
Did it? Nope.
Because
Underneath you still had that burning desire,
To find what you were lacking
And u did. .

Because,
We found love

- Tasean Massiah

MIA'S TRUTH

5/5/16

It's hard to say why it is I'd never done it. I usually say I think it's a weak way out, but I'd be lying if I said I never played with the idea and I wouldn't be the only one.

The truth? I don't think I ever could. Call it FOMO or maybe I'm way too curious, but I know for a fact there's something I'll miss that I'll wish I hadn't. Maybe not for me, but for my closest cousin, maybe my mom, or my dad. For me, that's enough to live for.

Of course maybe not.

I could hit some crazy turning point that makes this part of my life seem really laughable memory because things can change so much, just like that.

Things always do.

They already have.

This is my last year as a teen. Which means I have to close an entire chapter of my life, that has pretty much been all of it. Actually, an entire book and I honestly cant say I'mm mad about it.

This chapter and this book has meant literally *everything* to me and for that reason I know it's time to let it go. This is the time I can find all new things to mean something to me and more.

This book marked a long, hard, weird place in my life, but I know I'll be so much better because of it.

I still live with the hope that one day I'll find all the things I was waiting for and then some. I believe that when I do, everything I learned during this time will somehow be of some huge importance and I'll be even more grateful for the struggled that shaped me, nearly broke me, and made me stronger.

I think that's where all the strongest people come from.

UNCONVENTIONALLY
THE DAMN SAME

The same argument made about food could be made for ourselves if we look at food as a metaphor of our lives. We know how bad some of things we put in it are, but we still choose to. For what real reason though? Because other people are, because were told its worth it, because it seems cool? I have centered my life around trying to be and look different than anybody else. That's obviously difficult considering at least a thousand other people are still going to do the same things.

I dyed my hair red, got a bunch of random piercings I didn't need, and tried dressing in what I believed was my own style. It didn't take me long to realize that "my own style" wasn't even so much my own. In a weird way, my constant desire to be different was still me conforming. I was doing the same stupid things as everyone else so I was no better. I was just as obsessed with being my own person as I accused everyone else of being with looking like everyone else.

If I truly wanted to be different I would've basically had to shave my head, never wear makeup again, and dress myself with random household items like paper bags. That would never happen. I wanted to be my own person so bad, but at what expense, my own discomfort? That would bother me much more than it would bother anyone who looked at me. They'd simply call me try and go on about their day.

But id already caused myself discomfort. When I was young, like when I started writing this, I had long, thick, perfect hair and eyelashes. My skin was something to make babies cry. After years of dying my hair, it was damaged beyond recognition. Makeup had destroyed my eyelashes and skin. At this point, I had ended up back where I started but in worse condition.

I looked at myself as someone who thought she could run across a field of zombies unscratched after she'd already seen others be badly mauled. When I came out of the other side, nothing had changed except that I too was ripped apart. I probably would've been better off had I stayed but I still chose to place myself in a situation, I had ridiculed others for willingly participating in.

I learned and I think that's what's I needed. I learned that if I wanted to beat someone at their own game I should choose not to play at all. I should make my own game, with far simpler rules and fewer risks. A game where it would be ok to do whatever you want and call out other players on their cheats. I shouldn't force anyone to play but show them this game was far more fun.

I learned that if you can't beat them you should never join them. I learned to turn a game of Monopoly into a game of Bullshit, but catching and calling it out for just that. The goal was to put monopoly out of business.

NOW THE WHO? WHAT? WHEN?

Humans are the smartest living things known to man, yet we know so little.

I think about niches and minorities and the one I thing I belong to. The one with the people who see things for what they really are and are devastatingly effected by it.

Then I think about the "majorities." The number of people in the world that hear and see horrible things happening but allow them to continue out of fear and self-preservation.

I think the reason the world hasn't changed or gotten better is because there are more people like that than the former.

Then I also wonder what this world would be like if my minority was the majority.

People are dying every *eight* seconds and in that short time, my mind has already come up with a million questions about what kind of people they are ... or were.

They're people like us. The people at the bottom and sometimes, way too many times, it's the people *just* like me.

The people that think so deeply it drowns them because thinking like this isn't easy. It suffocates you until you have no air left.

The thing I'd labeled as severe anger management issues, I was only now realizing was my biggest and most important strength in this world.

I have a passion in me that turns me into a person that other people sometimes hate because she always speaks the truths they don't want to hear.

People sometimes hate me because I am passionate about myself, my life, but I am also extremely passionate about every single person who lives on this earth with me, even the ones that cast me aside.

I'm passionate about people who aren't even passionate about themselves and that may sound crazy but I completely mean it. People sometimes hate me because they don't truly know me, which I guess is ironic because you now know more about me than most people I've known my entire life but you don't even know my real name. Maybe it would all make more sense if you really knew me. Maybe you never will. What I do know is:

You know that I'm young and that sometimes it probably shows, but you don't know why that really matters.

You know some things about the people that raised me but you don't know the name they gave me.

You know some things about my life and how it changed me, but you don't really know the people in it.

You know that I've dealt with a disease that's made me question everything about myself, people, and the world I live in.

You know that sometimes I wasn't able to be strong and at times I questioned by very existence.

You know so much about be, but you don't know who *I am* and that's okay because one day, you will.

Printed in the United States
By Bookmasters